## THE TRANSCRIPTS

# THE WARLORD ERA

## LASZLO MONTGOMERY

The Warlord Era

By Laszlo Montgomery

ISBN-13: 978-988-8843-83-1

© 2024 Laszlo Montgomery

HISTORY / Asia / China

EB210

Published in Hong Kong by Earnshaw Books Ltd.

# CONTENTS

In this Part 1 episode, Laszlo presents some of the events from the Qing Dynasty during the 19th century that facilitated the rise of the Warlord Era. We'll also introduce the man many historians call, "The First Warlord", Yuan Shikai.

This time in Part 2 we focus on the rise and fall of Yuan Shikai and all the measures he took between 1911-1916. Many of Yuan's actions primed the pump for the Warlord Era that followed his sudden death in June 1916.

The saga continues as the demise of Yuan Shikai is followed by the rise of Duan Qirui and Feng Guozhang. The Beiyang Military machine begins to splinter into two main factions or cliques. In this episode, we will also hear about the exploits and imperial dreams of the Mafoo Warlord, Zhang Xun. And as the world mainly focused on the Great War in Europe, these two years of 1917-1918 were filled with many momentous events happening in Republican Era China.

The Beiyang Army Faction breaks up into these several "cliques." Their armies will battle each other for supremacy of the government. Hubei military governor Wang Zhanyuan will be examined as one of the textbook examples of how these generals evolved into warlords. Zhili Clique leaders Cao Kun and Wu Peifu will also be introduced.

# INTRODUCTION

The China History Podcast was launched in June of 2010. The original intention of the show was to offer American people a basic understanding of Chinese history. Recognizing a widespread lack of even the simplest awareness of Chinese history in the USA, Laszlo Montgomery used the relatively new medium of podcasting to make it convenient and easy for listeners to access the show snd satisfy their curiosity to learn about China.

Now more than twelve years later, The China History Podcast is listened to in more than a hundred countries with less than half of the listeners residing in the US. There are over two hundred hours of free content that introduces Chinese history from mythical to modern times. Besides popular Chinese imperial history and post Qing Dynasty history, the China History Podcast has presented hours of content focusing on the lives of Overseas Chinese and their rich history.

The show is listened to all over the world by English-speakers hungry for an entertaining and informative explanation of China's history delivered in an enjoyable non-academic style. So many listeners around the world are Chinese, many of them happy for an entertaining way to reconnect with their heritage.

For more than a decade there have been so many calls from listeners to provide the transcripts to the programs. They will do much to help listeners learn more about China. Laszlo is happy to work with Earnshaw Books to bring you the transcripts from selected shows of The China History Podcast. These will become a unique and enjoyable way to advance English understanding, perhaps re-learn some forgotten history and gain a foreigner's perspective of China's great history presented by someone who has appreciated Chinese culture since he was a small boy growing up in Chicago.

Laszlo Montgomery

# The Warlord Era
# Part 1

**THE TRANSCRIPTS**

## SUMMARY

In this Part 1 episode, Laszlo presents some of the events from the Qing Dynasty during the 19th century that facilitated the rise of the Warlord Era. We'll also introduce the man many historians call, "The First Warlord", Yuan Shikai.

## TRANSCRIPT

**00:00**   Hey everyone welcome back to another episode of the China History Podcast. Laszlo Montgomery here bringing you Part 1 in what is possibly shaping up to be one of the longest series ever in the history of the CHP. Both long and complicated. I don't know how many times this subject has been requested going back to 2010 but the drumbeat has been louder than usual these past few months.

**00:30**   Well, talk about complicated. The Warlord era involved more than a dozen cliques and a hundred warlords and their allies who dominated Chinese history from the year of Yuán Shìkǎi's passing in 1916 to the end of the Northern Expedition in 1928 and into the commencement of the Nanjing Decade.

**00:52**   We'll look at some of the history of the ill-fated Republic of China on the Chinese mainland as well as all the marquee warlords. You've heard their names many times before in this CHP program and in the course of your own China history studies: Duàn Qíruì, Wú Pèifú, Yán Xíshān, Zhāng Zuòlín, Zhāng Zōngchāng, Féng Yùxiáng, Cáo Kūn, Sūn Chuánfāng, Lǐ Zōngrén and so many others.

01:22 And all these cliques or factions that battled each other — the Ānhuī Clique, The Zhílì Clique, The Fèngtiān Clique, the Shānxī Clique, Guǎngxī Clique — over the next several episodes I'll sort everything out for you.

01:38 There were the Northern Warlords, the Southern Warlords, those in the Northwest and the Southwest. There are going to be a heck of a lot of names and I'm going to list the cast of characters mentioned in each episode in the show notes at the website and for those of you who are often throwing up your hands and sighing from getting tripped up by all the Chinese names, I'll try and sort everything out for you so that you don't get overwhelmed and swept out to sea.

02:06 We'll focus on no more than maybe ten warlords and their respective cliques. But plenty more will be mentioned in the telling of this history. The Eastern part of China will get more attention than the western part. I'll mention the Mǎ family in northwest China. Some of you remember the Xīběi Sān Mǎ episode CHP-78. The Warlord Ma Clique of Northwest China.

**02:32** You know, you can't tell the story of the Warlord Era without also mentioning all the background events happening concurrently in Republican Era history from 1911 to 1949. But at no additional cost whatsoever I'll provide you with as much background as necessary to tell the story of these warlord figures who didn't give the new post-Qing Dynasty government a chance. And thanks to their antics, China remained a weak and disorganized pushover for the European imperialist powers and Japanese militarists to take full advantage of. China's political and military disarray allowed a lot of countries and companies to feast on China's self-inflicted misfortune.

**03:21** These warlords were responsible directly and indirectly for tens of millions of deaths from all the grocery list of reasons that result in famine, disease and all manners of collateral damage to the populace from all the wars and battles fought. The patriotism of these warlords was always in question. Some were credited with being more patriotic than others. But their true loyalties were to their own selves first and foremost. Money and power. That's what mattered to them. Building a new China to stand up to the foreign powers all scrambling to get a piece of the beleaguered nation—not high on the list.

**04:03** So, although there has always been this great interest in China's warlord past and a hunger to know about their stories and escapades, the truth is, they were the cause of much of the worst suffering the Chinese nation would see in modern times. They made it easy for Japan to

come in and do all the terrible things they did to China and the Chinese people.

04:28 | The warlords made it near impossible for any semblance of a central government to emerge that could, you know, as we say in the Beautiful Country, establish justice, ensure domestic tranquility, provide for the common defense and promote the general welfare.

04:46 | In taking stock of every episode of the China History Podcast going back to 2010, I have to admit it's rather lopsided in terms of topics concerning PRC history vs. ROC history. For all of you patiently waiting for some Republican Era Chinese history, you did not wait in vain. I'm going to try and make up for that in this series.

05:09 | The thing is, in China during this warlord era of 1916 to 1928 when China was not unified, this wasn't anything new. Throughout the period of all the imperial dynasties, there were these times when China just fell apart. When the ancient Zhou Dynasty kings lost control of the feudal lords and their various fiefdoms, it ushered in a long period known as the Spring and Autumn and Warring States Eras. It was a bloody and violent time but paradoxically one of the most fruitful as far as the emergence of traditional Chinese culture was concerned.

05:47 | But we remember the Warlord Era most of all perhaps because it was so relatively recent and much fresher in our consciousness. This all went down in China merely a century ago. And we've been living with the consequences ever since. In any country's history everyone, for better or for worse, citizens of each nation, have been the beneficiaries or victims of their nation's history.

06:15 You really have to think hard to find some benefit to the Chinese masses that came out of this warlord era. After all the research I've done the past weeks and months, honestly I couldn't find any.

06:29 One irrefutable historical truth of China's warlord era was that it was a time of political, military, economic and social chaos. There's no "But such and such was a positive result of all the national suffering." No good came of their antics. There was no unexpected or unintended positive result that inadvertently happened that brought peace, happiness or prosperity to the masses. It was just one long agonizing period of suffering and lost opportunities for China.

07:05 So let's go back in time to see how the stage was set for this disastrous decade in Chinese history. These warlords just didn't appear out of nowhere. There was some historical background to their rise to power.

07:19 China's so-called Century of Humiliation, the Bǎinián Guóchǐ began with the Opium War. I've mentioned in past episodes how the Manchu Qing Dynasty sort of began to sputter sometime during the second half of the reign of the Qiánlóng Emperor, the longest reigning emperor in Chinese imperial history. Like a lot of leaders in world history, he lived too long and many of his early achievements were sort of negated by the decisions

5

made or not made when he kept on ruling after he was no longer at the top of his game.

**07:55** Where's a good place to start? The Taiping Rebellion is as good a place as any. Aside from everything else there is to say about this upheaval from 1850-1864 that led to something like twenty million deaths, it highlighted the abysmal state of affairs that existed in the Qing military. Besides this national cataclysm brought on by the Taiping rebels, the poor old Xiánfēng Emperor, during the early years of his depressing reign, had to deal with the Niǎn and Miáo Rebellions and the Second Opium War as well.

**08:30** When it was clear the Qing army wasn't going to be able to quash the Taiping rebels, they had to turn to what was, for all intents and purposes, a mercenary army to save China. Some were led by foreigners. But as far as the Warlord Era, all of the 20th century militarists who played any significant role in the warlord era owed their positions to the outcome of the Taiping Rebellion.

**08:57** The Xiánfēng Emperor needed help and he was left with no choice but to reach out to these provincial governors and have them act as his proxy to put an end to this national unrest. Two of the biggest names that rose to the fore were Zēng Guófān and Lǐ Hóngzhāng. Those two men had their own armies. Zēng Guófān commanded the Xiāng Army. Xiāng is just an abbreviation for Húnán. And Lǐ Hóngzhāng controlled the Huái Army of Ānhuī.

**09:28** These regional armies like the Hunan and Huái armies evolved from a kind of local militia called Yǒng Yíng armies. And these local militias were filled with peasant soldiers gathered from the province. Beside these two more well-known armies, the Hunan and Huai Armies, there were also others. This was the trend. By this time in Chinese history, 1850s and 1860s, the country had already fallen into the Imperialist trap and the Qing court were fated never to break free from that. And as a result of this, law and order broke down and true power gravitated to the regional governments.

**10:10** Building an army from the ground up is one of those more complicated than it looks kind of things. So in the case of building an army, as with building an addition on to your home, it's easier to call in a sub-contractor to manage the job for you. But unlike with building a new addition on to your home where you pay the contractor to do the work and he walks away, with these provincial armies, they stuck around.

**10:36** Pretty much from the year 1644 when they founded the Qing Dynasty, the Manchu rulers were fighting a losing battle. They were Manchus, which today is no big deal, but back then the majority Han Chinese population from the get-go, bristled at having to be subservient to them. And after two hundred years, mid-19th century, nothing had changed. When times were good during the first century of the Qing, everyone kept their mouth shut. But less than twenty years into the Century of Humiliation, the overwhelmingly non-Manchu portion of the population mostly concluded these guys did not

THE
CHP
CHINA HISTORY PODCAST
THE TRANSCRIPTS

THE WARLORD ERA
PART 1

have the Mandate of Heaven anymore and had to go.

11:20 And so... the Taiping Rebels went down in defeat, 1864, and the armies hired to put an end to them stayed. When Zēng Guófān died in 1872, his protege Lǐ Hóngzhāng, 49 at the time, took over as the most powerful military strongman in China as well as the dynasty's go-to guy for any matters relating to foreigners. And the more Lǐ Hóngzhāng got to know these foreigners, the greater he became convinced the foreigners and their weapons and technologies would be the key to China's defense and future survival.

12:00 Lǐ Hóngzhāng wasn't the only game in town. There were others as well who filled the vacuum left behind by the Qing ruler, whose powers were greatly diminished the farther you got from Beijing.

12:12 In 1871 the Běiyáng Army had been established as one of four modernized regional armies. This was the Qing Dynasty's great post-Taiping Rebellion hope for the future of their military. The Běiyáng Army grew to become the biggest and most powerful of them all. They were funded by Lǐ Hóngzhāng who was able to use his position of authority to funnel as much money as needed to buy ships and armaments from the Europeans.

12:42 Steamships, railroads, and telegraph service had arrived. Treaty ports weren't shantytowns anymore. The old days that moved no faster than the speed of a horse were gone forever. China's leaders were a deer in the headlights as soon as the 20th century approached.

**13:01** They had a lot of catching up to do. But in the meantime, such a rich and economically vibrant country as China with that one-of-a-kind population and market was just sitting there waiting to be plundered.

**13:15** The primary reason for China's urgency to shape up or ship out with their military was the outcome of the 1894-1895 First Sino-Japanese War. I want to mention the Běiyáng Fleet and their role in this debacle for China.

**13:31** Under Lǐ Hóngzhāng's leadership, the Běiyáng Fleet had grown, on paper anyway, to become one of the largest, most powerful navies in the world. But for a lot of reasons, poor training and corruption, it looked a lot better than it actually was. By the time of the Sino-Japanese War, this was practically the only significant fighting force that was equipped to take on the much better armed and trained Japanese navy.

**14:01** Despite the investment and all the training from foreign officers, the Běiyáng Fleet got their asses kicked in this war. And from 1895 on, the Běiyáng Fleet was never able to make a comeback and was ultimately merged with China's other navy to the south. Some of you might recall the story about how monies earmarked for the Běiyáng Fleet went instead to the building of the Empress Dowagers Marble pleasure boat.

**14:30** So, 1895, the Japanese military creams China and humiliates them internationally. This was followed by the disastrous Treaty of Shimonoseki. Thanks to this wake-up call, China was forced to go into hock to all

9

these European banks who couldn't issue bonds and other types of debt fast enough. That war indemnity China had to pay Japan was oppressive, as indemnities forced under duress are wont to be. With Japan on a roll and eyeing China's northeast, the dynasty was forced to keep them in check by letting the Russians into Manchuria in greater numbers at great territorial cost.

15:12 After the Treaty of Shimonoseki at the highest levels of power the rulers, political figures and military men all said now we're serious, let's finally stop talking about modernizing the military and really do it this time.

15:27 This is where the rise of the Běiyáng Army comes in. The whole Warlord Era owes its existence to this former Huái Army that had been created and built up by Lǐ Hóngzhāng. I just mentioned with money he was able to raise in the provinces he controlled, Lǐ Hóngzhāng built up the Běiyáng Army to become the most powerful and mighty of China's armies. Like the Běiyáng Fleet, the Běiyáng Army didn't perform all that well in the Sino-Japanese War. In fact so poor was their joint performance, that pretty much spelled the end to Lǐ Hóngzhāng's career.

16:06 Before Lǐ Hóngzhāng breathed his last in 1901, he got to be part of one more milestone in Chinese history. This was the handling of the Boxer Protocol that ended the Boxer Rebellion. He unwisely chose the side of the Empress Dowager in this uprising against all foreigners in China that didn't end well for the Middle Kingdom. With Li's passing shortly thereafter, it was going to be left up to his protege and successor Yuán Shìkǎi to be the next strongman in China.

16:39    Yuán Shìkǎi. He's sometimes called the first of the 20th century warlords.

16:46    After the Boxer Rebellion ended on September 7, 1901 it began a new era of China embracing all the West could offer, that was useful to the country, that is. This was the period of self-strengthening. With the dynasty now on its last legs, it also represented one final opportunity for the foreign powers to take one last bite out of that rotten apple of a dynasty.

17:14    Yuán Shìkǎi had gotten his start working for Lǐ Hóngzhāng. Yuan was an extremely energetic sort, very dependable and always got the job done. He was a man who, though short in stature, was long on real talent. His big start came back in 1885 when he was sent by Lǐ Hóngzhāng to Korea to represent China's interests there. The Japanese were just starting to ramp up in Asia and they were competing with China for influence there.

17:47    Yuan had been recalled back to China in 1894 right on the eve of the First Sino-Japanese War. One of the upshots of China's humiliating defeat was the formation of the New Army, the Xīn Jūn. Yuan had been put in charge of this project. The New Army played a starring role in suppressing the Boxers and protecting the besieged foreign powers in Beijing.

**18:13** What's important to know is that Yuán, through his control of this New Army, allied himself with the Qing court. Before the Boxer Rebellion, Yuán Shìkǎi had cozied up to the Empress Dowager, and he provided all the muscle needed to assist in putting an end to the Hundred Days Reform. That was in 1898. The Guangxu Emperor and his forty decrees that sought to modernize the country, written by King Youwei, Liang Qichao and others, were forty decrees too many as far as the Empress Dowager was concerned. So Yuán Shìkǎi and his New Army played a role in making sure that never happened. And thanks to this act, Yuan endeared himself to the Qing court.

**18:59** Yuán Shìkǎi kept using his energies and political skills to continue growing this army and on June 25, 1902 it was renamed the Běiyáng Army. This wasn't the only army in China. Not by a long shot. Every province had one. But Yuan's Běiyáng Army was the most powerful. And since they were up in Beijing and were primarily responsible for keeping the Qing Dynasty on life support, they had a rather unique role to play.

**19:31** Back then and all the way through the Warlord Era, whoever controlled Beijing, controlled the government. And whoever controlled the government, was first in line to deal with the foreign powers and to get access to their foreign capital.

**19:46** After Lǐ Hóngzhāng passed in 1901, Yuán Shìkǎi, in June 1902, replaced him as Viceroy of Zhílì, a post held previously by Zēng Guófān and then by Lǐ Hóngzhāng.

**20:01** Zhílì. You'll hear that word a lot in this series. It's a name for a province setup in the Ming and Qing dynasties. Zhílì translated means "directly subservient to." In today's China I guess you could sort of compare Zhílì to the municipalities who are physically located inside a province but report directly to the central authorities rather than to the governor. In our time, Beijing, Tiānjìn, Shànghǎi and Chóngqìng are four cities that don't have to answer to any provincial authority.

**20:37** Well, the same went with Zhílì province. They reported directly to the imperial government. Zhílì today comprises most of Hebei province, some of Henan and a piece of Shandong. Beijing was physically located inside the Zhílì region. That's why being the viceroy, or governor-general of Zhílì was a very key post. The fate of the dynasty rested in the viceroy's hands. In Chinese, the position was called the Zǒng Dū. There were eight viceroys in China.

**21:11** The term Běiyáng was used to name the areas along China's coast that was comprised of portions of Zhílì, Shandong and the northeast. Beijing, where the Qing government was located, was the center of it all. And whoever held the position of Viceroy of Zhílì, they were in charge of everything. The position of Běiyáng Tōngshāng Dàchén was held by the Viceroy of Zhílì and this post, known as the Minister of Běiyáng, was also in charge of trade relations and matters concerning foreign affairs.

21:46　Yuán Shìkǎi, after Lǐ Hóngzhāng's passing, wore all of these hats. He had already started to make a name for himself in Korea and had slowly built up his power working in Lǐ Hóngzhāng's shadow. Yuán had managed not to get too dirtied in the Sino-Japanese War and had made himself useful to the dynasty in the Hundred Days Reform. Now his biggest moment had arrived.

22:14　In 1903 Yuán Shìkǎi was in full military modernization mode. He built up six divisions of this new and improved Běiyáng Army. He employed Japanese and German military instructors and advisers to train officers. And later on, five of these officers being groomed would, in time, serve as either the president or premier of China. And a lot of the men who would play starring roles in the Warlord Era were just now being placed in various positions of power by Yuán Shìkǎi and he acted as a sort of godfather to the whole Běiyáng organization.

22:54　Believe it or not, there was a lot more going on in China than just the demise of Lǐ Hóngzhāng and the rise of Yuán Shìkǎi. I'm doing all I can to try not to wander too far from our central story. At the dawn of the 20th century, there's a whole slew of political figures all over China plotting for the downfall of the Manchu Qing Dynasty, Sun Yat Sen included. He had formed his Tóngménghuì or United League in 1905. This party was the forerunner to the Guomindang or KMT.

23:28　In November of 1908 the Empress Dowager Cixi finally died. John King Fairbank wrote, "The Manchu leadership left behind by the Empress Dowager was thoroughly unmemorable: a child emperor, a venal regent, vainglorious young princes, effete courtiers, all of them together just smart enough to inhibit change but quite incapable of leading it." In 1909, this Qing court, weary of his growing power, dismissed Yuán Shìkǎi as a threat to their existence as a ruling dynasty.

**24:07** They were right about that. On Double Ten Day, 1911, another major milestone in Chinese history, the Wǔchāng Uprising. Down in Hubei Province elements of the New Army rebelled against the Qing. And once that happened, within one and a half months fifteen provinces in China declared independence from the Qing. The Qing court looked to Yuán Shìkǎi to get them out of this jam, but he knew the dynasty was decades past its sell-by date and rather than keep them going, he cut a better deal with the revolutionaries trying to push China into the direction of a republic.

**24:45** And the rest is history. A history we will look at in the next installment of the CHP. I wanted to provide you with a short, to the point, overview of the events that led up to this moment. This sad and frustrating period in Chinese history has been discussed more than a few times in past episodes. I skipped over quite a bit but we'll come back again one day to zoom in on all the antics that went down all over China from the conclusion of the Taiping Rebellion to the end of the Qing Dynasty.

**25:17** Next episode, we'll pick up with the actual beginnings of the warlord era. In the beginning, as we saw, there was Zēng Guófān. And from Zēng Guófān came Lǐ

15

Hóngzhāng and Lǐ Hóngzhāng begat Yuán Shìkǎi. And as we'll see next time, the first generation of warlords all got their start as part of Yuán Shìkǎi's team. And this team was the entire Běiyáng organization that, in northern China at least, controlled the military and to a lesser extent, relations with the foreign imperialist powers. All for next episode.

25:56 Okay, me little beauties, that's all I got for all ya'lls this time. I don't know how many more episodes it's going to take to tell this story, but I do welcome you to come back next time and see how far we can go before the buzzer rings.

26:09 This is Laszlo Montgomery signing off from Los Angeles, Cali down here in the Southland. What a nice summer I had. Sorry to see it go. Do come back again next time and join me and millions of others all over the planet for another exciting episode of The China History Podcast.

## SUMMARY

This time in Part 2 we focus on the rise and fall of Yuan Shikai and all the measures he took between 1911-1916. Many of Yuan's actions primed the pump for the Warlord Era that followed his sudden death in June 1916.

## TRANSCRIPT

| | |
|---|---|
| 00:00 | Welcome back ladies and gentlemans to another CHP episode, Laszlo Montgomery here bringing you Part 2 in this long-requested series that will cover the main events and history of the Warlord Era in China, the one we remember most, that lasted from 1916 to 1928 and into the Nanjing Decade. |
| 00:24 | In the previous episode, we saw how these local Yŏng Yíng militias, often referred to as Braves, in Húnán and Ānhuī led by Zēng Guófān and Lǐ Hóngzhāng, came to the aid of the Qīng government and delivered to Hóng Xiùquán and his Tàipíng rebels the final knockout punches that ultimately led to the conclusion of that long and bloody civil war. |
| 00:53 | And after the venerable Zēng Guófān passed in 1872, it was his protege Lǐ Hóngzhāng who would lead the Qīng Dynasty's military modernization efforts, for better or |

for worse. And then we left off with the heir to all the military and diplomatic endeavors and achievements started by Lǐ Hóngzhāng. And this was Yuán Shìkǎi.

01:17 I mentioned that some historians call Yuán the first warlord. In a way he was. You can judge for yourselves. I mentioned last episode that he was one of Lǐ Hóngzhāng's people. He got his start in Korea and served there admirably for a decade. At first, he made himself useful to the Qīng royal court, helping Empress Dowager Cixi put an end to the 1898 Hundred Days Reforms of her nephew, the Guāngxù Emperor. Then he lined up against her during the Boxer Rebellion. And finally upon Cíxǐ's death in 1908, the Qīng royals sent Yuán Shìkǎi packing, fearful of his growing power and influence.

02:02 In between the time of his sacking up to the time of the October 1911 Wǔchāng Uprising on Double Ten Day, Yuán Shìkǎi was back in his home province of Hénán planning his next move. When the very survival of the dynasty was at stake, the Qīng royals went back to Yuán, cap in hand, and inquired if he'd be willing to come to their defense. His two main proteges who we'll hear all about next episode, Duàn Qíruì and Féng Guózhāng, they were his eyes and ears during this time and kept him informed about all the events he was missing out on.

02:41 And that's where we can pickup the story today and run with it. Yuán Shìkǎi was fifty-two years old at the time of the Wǔchāng Uprising, younger than me. In his role as the most powerful person in China thanks to his control of the Běiyáng Army and the Clique of generals and officers in that organization, he had a very strong negotiating position.

03:04 The Qīng government led by Empress Dowager Lóngyù, former empress consort to the Guāngxù Emperor, showered Yuán Shìkǎi with attractive offers. Keeping Yuán on their side, at this life or death moment for the Qing dynasty, was never more critical. When they were laying their limited number of cards on the table Yuán's army gave Sun Yat-sen and his followers a little pressure by taking back the cities of Hànyáng and Hànkǒu, two of the three cities that make up Wǔhàn. Wǔchāng was still in the hands of the revolutionaries. With Yuan taking this action, Sun didn't know for sure yet which side Yuán stood on.

03:46 So the Empress Dowager Lóngyù and her court knew their fate rested in Yuán's hands.

03:53 The southern revolutionary leaders whose main objective was the downfall of the Qīng, had no shortage of volunteers and supporters willing to fight for them. But the armies they cobbled together were weak and the soldiers had little or no training and besides all that, there weren't even enough rifles and bullets to go around. And because of the nature of their organization none of the foreign powers were willing to risk extending loans to these southern-based revolutionaries.

04:24 In late December 1911, a couple months after the Wǔchāng Uprising, Sun Yat-sen and his followers took stock of their situation and knew, for the sake of national unity, they had to start a dialog with Yuán Shìkǎi. Sun had said, "It is true that Yuán Shìkǎi is not trustworthy. Yet we can use him to overthrow the two hundred sixty year Manchu tyrannical rule. It would be better to do this than to launch a war by sacrificing over a hundred thousand troops to achieve the same goal." In other words better to cut a deal than risk all-out civil war with a very well-armed Yuán Shìkǎi and his Běiyáng Clique.

05:10 The one tasked by Sun Yat-sen to represent their interests was Lí Yuánhóng. You'll hear his name plenty in the episodes to come. He had already begun discussions with Yuán Shìkǎi in November 1911. Progress had been made but no solution was agreed to by the two sides. On December 18, 1911 a national assembly in Nánjīng was held to vote on the matter of president. Two days later on December 20, representatives from seventeen provinces voted and chose Sun Yat-sen as the first president of the Republic.

05; 46 And on New Year's Day 1912, Sun Yat-sen was sworn in. And just as Máo Zédōng would do a little over thirty-eight years later with the PRC, Sun Yat-sen declared the founding of the Republic of China.

06:02 But Sun and his Tóngménghuì 同盟会 or United League supporters knew they were too weak to stand up to Yuán. And being in a position to challenge Yuán and his Běiyáng Army was all wishful thinking. They had to give Yuán Shìkǎi a little more face than he was getting.

**06:20**  The fate of the Manchu royals up in Beijing was still in limbo. They were desperately trying to stay in the game but their fate rested entirely in Yuán Shìkǎi's hands. The child emperor and his regent the Empress Dowager Lóngyù had not yet abdicated. Sun Yat-sen proposed to Yuán, if you force the abdication, I'll pass the provisional presidency of the Republic on to you.

**06:48**  Yuán Shikai's sentiments leaned more in the direction of a constitutional monarchy. Given China's millennia old historical tradition of emperors, he was not alone in thinking this was a more appropriate form of government. Yuán truly believed, and I guess you could say rightly so, that a republic wasn't suitable for China and all it would do is lead to civil war and continued unrest. But beyond Yuán's core supporters there wasn't much excitement about keeping the emperor.

**07:21**  Yuán could have gone against the tide of history and tried to preserve the Great Qīng Dynasty, but rather than doing that he cut a better deal with the revolutionary leaders in the south.

**07:32**  And with a full court press of political pressure led by Yuán's right hand man Duàn Qíruì, on February 12th, 1912 the Last Emperor Pǔyí, abdicated. And a few days later Yuán Shìkǎi, as promised by Sun and his followers was elected the provisional president down in Nánjīng.

**07:56** This was the high point of the whole revolution. In the days and weeks that followed the mood in both Nánjīng where the revolutionaries were based, and up in Beijing, home turf of the Běiyáng Army was, in a word, ebullient. No one at that time knew anything about WWI or Japanese aggression in China, the Second Sino-Japanese War, WWII and the rise of the communists. All these things that defined early 20th century Chinese history — that was all beyond the horizon. Sun had expected that Yuán would take up his new leadership position in Nanjing where their government was based. But Yuán didn't take them up on the offer and said he'll run things from the north.

**08:42** For now, Yuán Shìkǎi was the man of the hour and from more than one source he was lionized as China's George Washington, the father of the country. Such heady times in early 1912. So much sweet-talking went on between Yuán Shìkǎi and Sun Yat-sen and their followers. But deep inside Sun knew a strongman such as Yuán was the best bad choice available and for the time being, they had to make it work. After all, the revolutionaries were happy. They wanted the end of the Qīng Dynasty and they got it.

**09:20** By the way, as part of the plan to push them over the edge and force an abdication, Yuán offered a very sweet deal to the royal family that allowed them to remain in the Forbidden City, receive a generous $4 million annual stipend and no one was allowed to molest or injure them. Considering what was usually the fate for overthrown monarchs, it wasn't a bad ending for them. Better than what the Romanovs got.

**09:49** The big winner by far was the Běiyáng Clique led by its leader Yuán Shìkǎi. He was now head of the Republic. Everyone on all sides was outwardly getting along and there was this feeling in the air that this Republic of China thing might work out after all. But as we'll find out, this turned out to be one of the biggest cases of Tóng Chuáng Yì Mèng in modern Chinese history. They all shared the same bed but both sides had completely different dreams.

**10:23** Almost from the outset there was trouble brewing. Yuán Shìkǎi was a military man and he knew very little about this new government system. As president he thought he was the main man. But under the current parliamentary system, the real power at the top was vested in the premier who, at the time, was Táng Shàoyí. You may recall, maybe not, he was a mentor to Wellington Koo and gave him his first big break and allowed him to marry his daughter. Wellington Koo, we looked at him in CHP episodes 214 and 15. Though Táng Shàoyí was close to Yuán, he quickly saw that Yuán didn't like being the number two guy.

**11:06** This is where everything started to go downhill. Within a couple months Táng Shàoyí threw in the towel and resigned as the first premier of the ROC. Yuán Shìkǎi was like a bull in a China shop. He did some good things. He did attempt some kind of political reconciliation and hoped to unify China. He promoted education and other reforms. But all the good Yuán Shìkǎi tried to promote…

all took a back seat to his top priority of consolidating his power. Over the next few years many of the big names of the warlord era will start to emerge as Yuán starts gaming the political system and slotting them in various government positions.

11:55 Financially Yuán Shìkǎi was in dire straits. The revenue coming into the country, after most of it was siphoned off to the foreign powers to pay for these loans and indemnities, was minuscule at best. China was getting by on foreign loans. The future was looking bleak and the honeymoon period between the coalition in the south led by Sun Yat-sen and Yuán in the north was a short one. And this was looking more and more like a shotgun wedding.

12:26 And after the KMT, founded by Sòng Jiàorén in August 1912 by joining together various competing factions, after they won big in the elections held at the end 1912, early 1913, the politically astute knew trouble was brewing. Sòng Jiàorén had more than a few enemies. Liáng Qǐchāo and Sun Yat-sen were certainly his rivals. Sòng represented a great hope for the KMT and perhaps for the future of his nation. Quite a charismatic guy and not a bad speaker.

13:03 After the heady victory of his party in the elections, Sòng Jiàorén railed particularly hard against Yuán Shìkǎi and how he was running roughshod over the new Republic of China government systems. Sòng knew the freshly minted KMT, even though they had a majority in the lower house of the National Assembly, was toothless before Yuán and his Běiyáng Clique. Lacking a more attractive option, Sòng at first opted to hold his nose and began to work with Yuán.

**13:37**   But Yuán knew Sòng Jiàorén, this ambitious young firebrand of a revolutionary, so politically astute, so filled with energy and patriotism and so committed to democratic principles, was politically nothing but a threat to him. And for this reason, although it was never proven beyond the shadow of a doubt, Yuán Shìkǎi green-lighted the assassination of Sòng Jiàorén. March 20, 1913, definitely a date that will live on in Chinese historical infamy, at 10:40 PM on a train platform in Shanghai. One shot from behind was all it took. Sòng Jiàorén died two days later.

**14:23**   Just before he took his final breath, Sòng had written a letter to Yuán Shìkǎi saying, "I die with deep regret. I humbly hope that your Excellency will champion honesty, propagate justice, and promote democracy." The suspects in the assassination all died mysteriously or disappeared. Plenty of people benefitted from Sòng Jiàorén's death but all the leads pointed to Yuán Shìkǎi. No one had ever found the smoking gun that tied Yuán to Song's death, but he had the most to gain with Sòng Jiàorén out of the way.

**15:03**   The great Gady Epstein in his December 2012 piece for the Economist, a pdf of which I keep on my hard drive just for moments like these, called Yuán"… the cartoon villain of this tale, with bushy mustache, round open face and slightly overfed build of an indulged monarch."

It was clear by now that there were two things Yuán Shìkǎi did not want: A premier who could challenge him in the government and a constitution that would tie his hands and limit his powers. He was no George Washington.

**15:40** Well, so much for that. It was barely more than a year between the time of five-year old Emperor Pǔyí's abdication and Sòng Jiàorén's assassination. All that heady talk and high hopes for Yuán Shìkǎi to become this leader he was never meant to be. All that went out the window.

**16:01** On April 26, 1913 Yuán inked a foreign syndicated loan of twenty-five million pounds sterling. And he went right over the head of the parliament and signed it himself. And where do you think that twenty-five million quid ended up? It all went to bolstering the Běiyáng Clique enterprise, directly and indirectly.

**16:24** The KMT, the Nationalist Party, the one formed by Sòng Jiàorén, revolted against Yuán and his Běiyáng Clique. And from July to September 1913 civil war broke out. Many of the provinces declared independence from the Běiyáng government. Ānhuī, Jiāngxī, Guǎngdōng, Húnán. And this event was called The Second Revolution. The Èrcì Gémìng. It was the revolutionaries of the south led by Sun Yat-sen and their military allies who also had an axe to grind with Yuán Shìkǎi, joining forces in an attempt to defeat the Běiyáng Clique.

17:03 | They may have performed poorly against Japan in the first Sino-Japanese War, but against these armies to the south, the Běiyáng Army swatted these revolutionary forces down in no time at all.

17:16 | And now everything was out in the open. All this animosity that existed on both sides. What a difference a year can make. Sun Yat-sen, knowing correctly that Yuán Shìkǎi wasn't going to take kindly to this uprising, fled the country in August and set himself up in exile in Japan, planning his next move.

17:39 | On November 4th, 1913 someone we'll be hearing more about in Part 3, future warlord Zhāng Xūn, After he took back Nanjing to effectively end The Second Revolution, he later got the okay from the top levels of the Beiyang organization to pillage and plunder the city. And in that month Yuán Shìkǎi called for the KMT to be dissolved.

18:04 | So January 1914 was a mini-Great Leap Forward as far as the stage getting set for the Warlord Era. Yuán shuttered the National Assembly. No dictators like having those around. And to place a fig leaf over the reality of his new strongman rule, Yuán put a sixty-five man congress or committee or whatever you wanna call it in place that looked and acted like a representative body except that everyone represented Yuán Shìkǎi. On May 1, 1914 Yuán annulled the 1912 Provisional Constitution.

18:42 | And his new version of the constitution gave him a little more elbow room as far as dictatorial powers went. Yeah, pretty much everything that had been put in place to get democracy up and running in China was deconstructed. And Yuán changed the term of president to ten years with no term limits. If Yuán Shìkǎi wanted to become president for life it was all up to him.

19:08 In each and every province Yuán put in place these Dūdu's who were military governors in charge of civil administration. And each of these military governors were all beholden to Yuán Shìkǎi. And by nurturing this system of putting all his hand-selected military officers in place in every province, this turned out to be one more brick in the wall as far as the establishment of warlordism in China.

19:40 And everyone who had argued since the time of the Guāngxù emperor that a republican form of government would never be able to get off the ground in China were proven right. Yuán had effectively turned himself into an emperor, which sort of got him thinking.

19:56 Well, 1915. What a year that was in China. January 18, the Japanese threw the Twenty-One Demands in China's face. We've discussed that more than a few times in the past. What Yuán Shìkǎi ended up signing on May 9th of that year had the worst of Japan's gimme's excised from the Twenty-one Demands agreement. But it was still pretty bad. After the ink was dry, Yuán Shìkǎi's PR team had a lot of explaining to do.

20:25 Right here with the signing of Japan's Twenty-one Demands is where anti-Yuán Shìkǎi sentiment starts to catch fire nationally. And not only with Yuán, with this act, forcing the Twenty-one Demands on China, even in its diluted final form, with this act, Japan took that first major step that would cause a sea change in anti-Japanese sentiments in China. And some could argue that sentiment is still smoldering today a hundred and four years later.

21:01 And the previous year, on June 28, 1914 Archduke Franz Ferdinand and his Mrs, gunned down in Sarajevo. We all know what happens in the wake of that. So now, amidst the wreckage of the failed Republic of China, the Twenty-one Demands and Yuán Shìkǎi's power plays, now we have World War One playing in the background. A terrible distraction for the European powers in China. A blessing for the Japanese, though.

21:31 All this history we've discussed a few times before, let's talk about the stuff that laid the groundwork for the Warlord Era.

21:38 There's really two more chapters in this epic saga to go before the horses rush out of the starting gate and it's every warlord for himself. The first, of course, is Yuán Shìkǎi's ill-advised attempt at restoring the monarchy with himself as emperor. Many credit, or give too much credit, to the American Frank Goodnow for being the one who put this bug in Yuán's ear about declaring himself emperor.

22:05 Goodnow had come to China with the backing of the Carnegie Endowment and a recommendation from the former president of Harvard. And he was sent to Beijing to be an advisor to Yuán Shìkǎi for the drafting of that new constitution, the one that opened the door to no term limits for the president, i.e. Yuán Shìkǎi.

22:26 But as far as his place in Chinese history, what we remember Frank Goodnow for was his assertion that Democracy had no place in China. The country still had a long way to go. Goodnow had arrived in Beijing only six weeks after Sòng Jiàorén's assassination and only saw the aftermath which involved a lot of protests and riots. Based on this experience, Goodnow said China was more suited to monarchy.

22:55 And though he didn't whisper into Yuán's ear that he should really consider making himself emperor of China, it was very nice and respectable justification and Yuán surely took it to heart. And so we got one step closer to the Warlord Era when Yuán Shìkǎi, end of 1915, declared his intention to form a new dynasty and proclaim himself emperor of China.

23:21 That decision, to put it mildly, was a mistake. All of the authoritarian measures Yuán had instituted, changing the constitution, outlawing the KMT, sidelining political rivals, this had already caused a deep division in the country. And now this.

23:41 Well, Yuán Shìkǎi, or the Hóngxiàn Emperor as he was called after the accession rites were held on New Years Day 1916, couldn't pass out peerages fast enough to all his supporters and hangers-on. All the military leaders and future warlords who we'll discuss in coming episodes were made princes, dukes, marquesses, counts, viscounts and barons. The whole thing could be summarized in a single word: shambolic. Yuán didn't have long to live but he lived long enough to regret this decision.

24:20    Even his subordinates at the top rungs of the military thought Yuán went a bridge too far with this whole emperor thing. The most immediate upshot of this instant debacle for Yuán was the National Protection War, the Hùguó Zhànzhēng.

24:37    It all started way down in the southwest in Yúnnán province. Three generals there who ran the province, Táng Jìyáo, Cài È, and Lǐ Lièjūn, on Christmas Day 1915, all declared independence from Yuán's government and went on the offensive. In the meantime, the two adjacent provinces to Yúnnán, namely Guìzhōu and Guǎngxī – same thing. They broke free and rose up against Yuán. Then as soon as the provinces of Guǎngdōng, Shāndōng, Húnán, Shānxī, Jiāngxī and Jiāngsū threw their lot in with the National Protection Army as it was called, Yuán Shìkǎi knew he miscalculated.

25:23    On March 22, 1916 on what would have been Sòng Jiàorén's thirty-fourth birthday, Yuán Shìkǎi abdicated and called the whole thing off. This smart move defused matters with respect to the National Protection War. Even some of Yuán's own Běiyáng generals had exhibited much diminished enthusiasm in their encounters with National Protection Army forces. After all it wasn't clear what was in it for them as far as their personal power base with Yuán ruling as emperor rather than as an old-fashioned military dictator.

**26:00**  But the southern military strongmen, they had had enough of this whole failed experiment and pretending to cooperate with Yuán Shìkǎi and his Běiyáng Clique. From here on out, they turned their backs on any calls for national unity.

**26:17**  This really complicates the telling of our story, this northern and southern split. For the rest of this series there were always multiple narratives happening and all their individual histories all played out at the same time and were intertwined here and there. What a video game this would make with an epic cast of potential characters. The warlords of north China, eastern China, southwest China, in the northwest.

**26:47**  Then on the 6th of June 1916, Yuán Shìkǎi died. Suddenly. Just like that. And that system he had put in place and nurtured with all these dūdu's, these military governors all in place, there was no longer one ring to rule them all, to use a well-worn metaphor.

**27:10**  And so we arrive at what most history books call the actual starting point of the Warlord Era: the death of Yuán Shìkǎi. It all began here with Yuán's death where, even though his prestige was diminished by the whole emperor fiasco, the signing of the 21 Demands, the civil war that was ramping up, he didn't have too much to show for as far as accomplishments over the past few years. Regardless, he held everything together using the traditional system of personal relationships with military governors he placed throughout the provinces in China within his political and military reach. It worked in the Zhou Dynasty. Still worked three thousand years later.

**27:56** Some of those guys out in the provinces with their weapons and soldiers, they had ambition too. And with Yuán gone, a bunch of them are going to test the limits of their greed and authority over their various territories of China. And next episode we'll pick up right there. Exit Yuán Shìkǎi and enter Duàn Qíruì, Féng Guózhāng and a host of others.

**28:23** That's it for now. My eternal thanks if you lasted this far. This is Laszlo Montgomery signing off from Los Angeles Califor-nee-i-a...Warlord Era part 3 coming next time. You can put that in the bank and start earning interest on that today. So please do join me then, same bat time, same bat channel, for another exciting episode of the China History Podcast.

# The Warlord Era
## Part 3

**THE TRANSCRIPTS**

## SUMMARY

The saga continues as the demise of Yuan Shikai is followed by the rise of Duan Qirui and Feng Guozhang. The Beiyang Military machine begins to splinter into two main factions or cliques. In this episode, we will also hear about the exploits and imperial dreams of the Mafoo Warlord, Zhang Xun. And as the world mainly focused on the Great War in Europe, these two years of 1917-1918 were filled with many momentous events happening in Republican Era China.

## TRANSCRIPT

| | |
|---|---|
| 00:00 | Welcome back again everyone. So happy you made time for me. Laszlo Montgomery here with Part 3 of this little CHP overview of the Warlord era in China 1916-1928. |
| 00:17 | We left off last episode in the year 1916 with the death of Yuán Shìkǎi. It couldn't have come at a more inopportune time. WWI was still raging in Europe. The foreign powers, Great Britain, France, Germany and the United States, were all tied up dealing with this, up till that time, most terrible of all wars. Although Japan wasn't exactly given a free hand in China, they sure were starting to act like they had one. |
| 00:47 | At this critical juncture in history when China could have gotten things together and used the events of WWI |

to their advantage. Things just went from bad to worse. And for the next twelve years a lot of suffering is going to be felt in China's cities, towns and villages.

01:08    Let's look at what happened in China immediately following the death of Yuán Shìkǎi. The men who first tried to step into Yuán's large-sized shoes were Duàn Qíruì and Féng Guózhāng. I thought we could hold these two up to the light and use Duàn and Féng as prisms to recount the events that unfolded in the summer of 1916 and into 1917.

01:35    Over on the European continent, as Yuán Shìkǎi was laid to rest, the Battle of Verdun was happening in northeast France. About 300,000 troops died in that battle. These new weapons and armaments that had emerged at the dawn of the 20th century were proving to be frightfully devastating. There will be quite a demand in China for a lot of these weapons of war after the Treaty of Versailles.

02:01    Duàn Qíruì was born and raised in the capital of Ānhuī province, Héféi. He remained associated with this province throughout his life and career. He had a halfway decent pedigree, having a grandfather who fought with Lǐ Hóngzhāng and his Huái Army. Lǐ Hóngzhāng by the way, was also born and raised in Héféi. Ānhuī province was always the central power base of Duàn Qíruì but as we'll see, he also served in a number of positions in the Republic of China government.

02:35    Almost every northern warlord I am going to mention from here on out got their start in some shape or form due to their relationship with Yuán Shìkǎi. Duàn Qíruì and Féng Guózhāng were no exception. They were both direct beneficiaries of Yuán's rise to the top of the political and military food chains in China.

02:57  Like I said, Duàn came from this military family and he went straight into a military career by way of the Tiānjìn Military Academy, one of the many of such kinds of institutions put in place by Lǐ Hóngzhāng, this one in 1885, in his efforts to modernize and organize China's military.

03:20  In the course of the early part of Duàn Qíruì's career in Shāndōng he got himself noticed by Lǐ Hóngzhāng. Lǐ sent Duàn to Germany for two years to go learn from the best. For military science, Germany and Japan were the two top places at the end of the 19th century for an aspiring Chinese militarist to learn a thing or two.

03:46  Duàn came back to China and went straight into the Běiyáng military organization and made his way up to the rank of military commander in Yuán Shìkǎi's personal pet project, the New Army. You recall the New Army from Part 1, After China's disastrous showing in the Sino-Japanese War, the building of this Xīn Jūn, New Army, was among the top priority military reform efforts of the Qing Dynasty.

04:14  Duàn stood right by Yuán Shìkǎi's side in Shāndōng province during the Boxer Rebellion. Yuán was serving there as the provincial governor. Duàn Qíruì saw action during this uprising that would later prove so

37

devastatingly costly to China. Duàn Qíruì was then able to parlay this feather in his cap into a command of his own division in the Běiyáng Army.

04:41 Then in 1906 things really began to gel for Duàn Qíruì. In these dying days of the Qīng, the Qīngcháo mòniándé mònián if you will, Duàn was given a plum posting at the Bǎodìng Military Academy 保定军校. In its day, this was the West Point of China, the top military training center, founded by none other than Yuán Shìkǎi.

05:07 This Bǎodìng Military Academy served as the model for the later Whampoa Military Academy down in Guangzhou. Chiang Kai-shek's later rise to the top of the ROC government is said to have started as the head guy at Whampoa. And Chiang took a page out of Duàn Qíruì's playbook later on when by using his position as Commandant at the Whampoa Military Academy to incubate a sizable coterie of followers who would all play central roles in the warlord years. Duàn did the same thing while heading the Bǎodìng Military Academy.

05:45 The Ānhuī Clique as it came to be known, really started to take shape right around here. Duàn used his positions to assemble quite an impressive number of officers and loyal supporters. And Yuán Shìkǎi had fortified his relationship with Duàn Qíruì by arranging a marriage between Duàn and his niece. So you can see why Duàn Qíruì, as soon as Yuán dies, is the natural choice for *capo de capo* of the Běiyáng military organization.

06:18    Duàn continued to benefit from Yuán Shìkǎi's rise. He was appointed the military governor of Húběi province. And then came the Wǔchāng Uprising and the Xīnhài Revolution 辛亥革命, 1911, all discussed briefly last episode in Part 2.

06:35    It wasn't all roses between Yuán and Duàn. After the revolution and after the trauma of agreeing on the first provisional government for the ROC in 1912 Duàn was made Minister of War in Yuán Shìkǎi's cabinet. He still ran Húběi. Starting from about here, Yuán and Duàn disagreed on many things. And Duàn Qíruì, I guess you can say right about now, using his powerful cabinet position of Minister of War sort of tries to became his own man and come out from behind Yuán Shìkǎi's shadow.

07:15    During Yuán's ill-fated run for the emperorship, he had sacked Duàn Qíruì as military governor down in Húběi as well as from his position as Minister of War. Yuán also went to the trouble to clean house in the Běiyáng upper echelons of any Duàn Qíruì allies that Duàn had put in place.

07:37    But in the end, after his bid to make himself emperor fizzled, Yuán Shìkǎi had to swallow his pride and rely on Duàn Qíruì to act as the mediator between himself and the rest of the country who had all lined up against him on this ill-conceived idea.

07:55    Then with Yuan's passing, his vice president Lí Yuánhóng, took over as president. And Duàn Qíruì, according to the terms of Yuán Shìkǎi's will, took over as premier. The parliament that Yuán Shìkǎi had dissolved in 1914 was put back together by August 1916. Duàn could hardly mask his disappointment at Lí Yuánhóng, who in his role as president was trying to govern rather than act as Duàn Qíruì's stooge.

08:18   Duàn Qíruì had basically the same mindset as his one-time mentor Yuán Shìkǎi. As most world leaders will generally concur, it's a lot easier to do your job in the capacity of a dictator rather than within the limitations of a democracy. And that's how Duàn liked to run things, from the top down. And this included the signing of the so-called Nishihara Loans with Japan that came to haunt China at the Treaty of Versailles. About $90 million in loans, mostly to be utilized by Duàn's Ānhuī Clique, in exchange for a rather free hand in railroad construction and management in Shandong, Manchuria and Mongolia.

09:11   The hope was that north and south could reconcile and pick up where they left off before Yuán Shìkǎi started becoming so autocratic. But this wasn't meant to be, and squabbles remained about — what else — sharing of political power. It was as serious back then as it is today. And China in the post-Yuán Shìkǎi period had one power base in the north led by this Běiyáng Clique and in the south led by the KMT, the Guómíndǎng. The West, I won't get into that right now.

09:45   And not only were the Běiyáng Clique leaders starting with Duàn Qíruì at loggerheads with the KMT, even within the Běiyáng government itself things were not terribly collegial.

**09:58** Before we discuss the Ānhuī-Zhílì rivalry, let me also introduce Féng Guózhāng. As I said, Féng Guózhāng was another Yuán Shìkǎi man who rose up the ranks and like Duàn Qíruì, got to use the Bǎodìng Military Academy as a breeding ground to groom his own followers.

**10:18** Unlike Duàn Qíruì who came from a military family, the army was not Féng Guózhāng's first choice for a career. He was a failed scholar who had taken the path of the civil bureaucracy. But he was never able to pass the exam that might have opened the door to that life for him. Instead, he turned to the military and never looked back.

**10:42** Féng Guózhāng, born and raised in Héběi province, which back then was known as Zhílì. You remember Zhílì from Part 1.

**10:53** He was also very close to Yuán Shìkǎi and had been part of the gang that forced the Qīng emperor Pǔyí to abdicate. He had remained very loyal to Yuán Shìkǎi and played key roles during the aftermath of the Wǔchāng Uprising.

**11:10** Like Duàn Qíruì and everyone else in China, Féng lined up against Yuán Shìkǎi when he tried to make himself emperor. Even his best friends and closest allies wouldn't support him. To show he meant business, Féng Guózhāng had left the north and headed to the KMT

THE
CHP
CHINA HISTORY PODCAST
THE TRANSCRIPTS

THE WARLORD ERA
PART 3

stronghold of Nánjīng to fight in the anti-Yuan National Protection War that I mentioned last episode.

11:36 And now in 1917, Féng Guózhāng found himself serving as Vice President of the Republic of China, second in command to the president, Lí Yuánhóng.

11:49 Féng and Duàn used their positions of political and military power and authority to stuff their offices with loyal followers. Féng, coming from Zhílì and all, hand selected officers and staff who all came from that province.

12:06 And Duàn Qíruì, an Ānhuī man, put together an organization that mostly came from Ānhuī.

12:14 So you can probably guess which one headed the Zhílì Clique and which one the Ānhuī Clique. You had the umbrella Běiyáng Clique organization formerly headed by Yuán Shìkǎi. And then after he's gone, Féng and Duàn split into two separate cliques with two separate armies.

12:37 Let me just mention one more warlord from this period. I mentioned him last time in Part 2. This was Zhāng Xūn. And 1917 was a big year for this man known as both the Mafoo Warlord and the Pig-Tailed General among other epithets. Zhāng Xūn was actually a few years older than Yuán Shìkǎi and had fought in the Sino-French War 1884-85. He had come from nothing from a town just west of Nánchāng in Jiāngxī province. He was called the Mafoo General because he had once worked as a Mǎfū, a kind of horse groom. Very humble beginnings.

13:20 And as far as his being called the Pigtailed General. That was the main thing about Zhāng Xūn. He was extremely loyal to the Qīng dynasty. A very ultra-conservative, traditionalist, through and through. In fact one of his early claims to fame had been that he was the one who escorted the Empress Dowager Cíxǐ and her entourage to safety when they had to flee the Forbidden City at the end of the Boxer Rebellion. So he was loyal to the Qīng and, even after the revolution in 1911 refused to cut off his queue. And soldiers that were under his command, he forbade them to cut off their queues as well.

14:00 Despite the republican times they lived in, Zhāng Xūn, this reactionary and dyed in the wool royalist, he flew the flag in China as chief defender of pre-revolutionary values and institutions.

14:14 Despite all this, he remained a staunch and reliable ally of Yuán Shìkǎi and had served him well at a few key moments, particularly, as I said, in crushing the KMT forces who fought back during the Second Revolution, June to November 1913. I mentioned last episode, you may recall, another one of The Mafoo Warlord's claims to fame, after Nánjīng was taken, Zhāng Xūn sat back and allowed his troops to have three days of looting and a whole lot more throughout the city.

14:49 He didn't line up with Yuán Shìkǎi when he did the whole emperor thing, but he remained neutral while everyone in the north and south had their knives out. You'd think he would have backed Yuán but Zhāng

Xūn's loyalty was to the Qing dynasty. So he couldn't support Yuán's bid for the emperorship.

15:07    He was a powerful military men and had a lot of fighting power. So with Yuán out of the way starting in 1916, Zhāng Xūn had his own ideas about what was best for China. Fellow militarists of like mind formed an Association of Provincial Military Governors. This became the main voice of the warlords. Zhāng Xūn took the lead in calling for the first of three conferences to be held comprised of all these generals and future warlords. All of these conferences were held in the historic city of Xúzhōu in northern Jiāngsū where it meets the borders of Ānhuī and Shāndōng.

15:52    The first meeting was held on June 9, 1916, a few days after Yuán died. There were representatives from seven of the northern provinces. How to handle the post-Yuán era was a topic of high priority. The second conference was held on September 20th, a few months later. This one was attended by representatives from twelve provinces, all the military top brass. In a moment of solidarity they all agreed to form a "Grand Alliance" amongst themselves and made Zhāng Xūn the "Great Leader" of the alliance. The group was comprised of all the deciders for any key decision that required central government approval.

16:36    These militarists, though it wasn't their place, began to speak out about which political leaders selected to serve in the government were suitable or not. In January 1917 there was a third Xúzhōu Conference held. By the time of this conference, everyone was jumping into the political arena. The rift that existed between Duàn Qíruì, representing the militarists, and Lí Yuánhóng representing the central government started to grow. The biggest bone of contention at this post-Yuán Shìkǎi moment concerned China's position on declaring war on Germany and joining the allies or remaining neutral.

17:20     Lí Yuánhóng wanted to stay out of the conflict. Duàn Qíruì, with Japan lobbying him like crazy, was all for declaring war on Germany. This was the most immediate cause for the current political crisis in Republican China. The Běiyáng leaders led by Duàn Qíruì, after dissolving parliament on June 12, 1917, were all huddled together in Tiānjìn in June, leaving Lí Yuánhóng with a feeling of uncertainty, I guess you could say.

17:52     Once Lí Yuánhóng had gotten wind of Duàn Qíruì's perfidy in signing the Nishihara loans and opening up China's front door and letting Japan inside so to speak, he canned Duàn as premier. So that's why Duàn was now hunkering down in Tiānjìn with all his military allies planning his response. He was putting Lí Yuánhóng's feet to the fire forcing him to see the light.

18:19     So with all these army generals and commanders not too far away from the capital rattling their sabers, Lí Yuánhóng, recognizing that might makes right, invited Zhāng Xūn to come to Beijing to broker a solution between his government and the military leaders lining up against him.

45

18:40 | So I've told you a few of the historic moments in Zhāng Xūn's life. But this one really takes the cake. Along with that whole business of keeping his hair Manchu style, complete with queue and being a rather colorful character, when he got to Beijing with his troops, rather than do what Lí Yuánhóng asked to do, broker a solution to the political impasse, he tried to restore the Qīng Dynasty instead.

19:06 | Zhāng Xūn had not only declared the restoration of the Qīng, as part of the deal he called for the return of all Qīng imperial institutions. He thought, or was led to believe, his fellow Běiyáng military generals were okay with this whole Qīng restoration thing. But just like with Yuán Shìkǎi and his monarchical dreams, the support that the Mafoo General was counting on from his fellow warlords wasn't there. This Manchu Restoration of 1917 lasted July 1 to July 12. Pǔyí got to be The Last Emperor not once, but twice.

19:50 | But then right after Zhāng Xūn pulled the trigger on this restoration, Duàn Qíruì and his other Běiyáng allies started making deals with Lí Yuánhóng, obviously under great duress. And before you knew it, Duàn Qíruì was returned to the government as premier and fellow Běiyáng stalwart Féng Guózhāng was installed as acting president. Lí Yuánhóng was out.

20:15 | Once everyone shook hands on this new arrangement, Duan, on behalf of all his military allies, ordered troops to head in the direction of Beijing. Mere moments before, Duàn and Li Yuanhong were at each other's throats.

Now they on the side of the Republic. And then they proceeded to quickly quash this whole bad idea of a Qīng Restoration before it could even catch fire.

20:43   Zhāng Xūn ended up fleeing with his troops and had to lay low for the rest of his life. He was pardoned in 1918 but you don't hear much of him after that. He died on 9-11 1923. He was marginalized early on in the warlord era but sure left his mark on early ROC history.

21:04   Here is where things start to get real complicated, if they weren't complicated enough already. Things really start to break down from this point forward. The central government of the Republic of China was nothing more than the government of whichever warlord seized and occupied Beijing. Whatever government officials and politicians serving in Beijing, they remained puppets of the warlord du jour. You'll see between now and the final buzzer, Beijing is going to change hands as warlords contend for this most important of cities.

21:42   Pretty much after Zhāng Xūn's big moment attempting to restore the Qing Dynasty, everyone who hadn't taken a side yet started taking sides. And any warlords and military governors in other parts of China, if they didn't want to be part of these Běiyáng generals and their puppet state they just declared their province independent and if the north wanted to force them into unifying with their government they could come down and try and make them.

47

**22:12**  So this whole Zhāng Xūn Manchu Qing Restoration move really kicked the hornets' nest so to speak. The way everything ended up in the immediate fallout it was a sort of coup d'état with the Zhílì and Ānhuī Cliques in control of things. In the north anyway. I haven't even gotten started on what was happening south of the Yangzi. They had plenty of warlords too.

**22:36**  Then on August 14, 1917, with Lí Yuánhóng, his primary opposition out of the way, Duàn Qíruì declared war on Germany and Austria. The Chinese Labor Corps, who we looked at in episode CHP-207, had already been serving in Europe for a year. And a month later, after Duàn's declaration of war, down in Guǎngzhōu, Sun Yat-sen — remember him? He setup a rival Chinese government. It didn't get much recognition, but he continued to keep that KMT flame alive down in the south.

**23:15**  Vice-president of China and warlord Féng Guózhāng made a sincere effort to become a peacemaker between the Northern and Southern governments. Unfortunately he wasn't fated to live long and died in Beijing in December 1919. This is going to shake things up in the Zhílì Clique that he led. Two warlords will emerge to take over from Féng Guózhāng.

**23:39**  You can see how this warlord problem keeps dividing and growing. From Yuan came Duan and Feng. From Feng came two more warlords who we will look at next episode.

**23:50** Yuán Shìkǎi, Duàn Qíruì, Féng Guózhāng, Zhāng Xūn. These were all the first generation warlords, the ones who occupied the stage during that critical juncture in Chinese history when the Revolution was launched and the Qing Dynasty fell. Their solution to the setting up of a new nation was always a military solution. And still, up to now, this whole Republic of China idea had been an abysmal failure.

**24:20** So you can see why, when Zhāng Xūn tried to restore the Qīng, he actually had a lot of support from a wide segment of the population who had had enough with this failed experiment in democracy and constitutional government.

**24:39** Rather than introduce what happened next, why don't we just say class dismissed a little early. Part 4 coming next time. Now things really get messy. You won't want to miss it. This is Laszlo Montgomery coming to you from the Southland once again. Los Angeles, California in the Golden State. Please join me next time, won't you, for another exciting episode of the China History Podcast.

## SUMMARY

The Beiyang Army Faction breaks up into these several "cliques." Their armies will battle each other for supremacy of the government. Hubei military governor Wang Zhanyuan will be examined as one of the textbook examples of how these generals evolved into warlords. Zhili Clique leaders Cao Kun and Wu Peifu will also be introduced.

## TRANSCRIPT

**00:00** Welcome back ladies and gentlemans, Laszlo Montgomery here with another edition of the China History Podcast.

**00:09** Warlord Era Part 4 this time. 1917-1918-1919. Such tumultuous times in the fledgling Republic of China. Man, they were making the Qīng Dynasty look good. We left off last time in the aftermath of the failed attempt by the Pig-Tailed General, Zhāng Xūn, at restoring the Qīng emperor onto the Dragon throne.

**00:33** In the wake of this shakeup Duàn Qíruì was made premier and chief decider in the government. And the warlord from Zhílì province Féng Guózhāng, he became the new president, succeeding Lí Yuánhóng who was far from his power base in the middle Yángzǐ down south. He couldn't stand up to these generals anymore than you or I could.

00:56 So August 1917, two warlords in charge of the government. For four months anyway. And from that point forward, it will be a revolving door in the offices of president, vice president and premier.

01:11 Down in the south of China, Dr. Sun Yat-sen set up a rival government based in Guǎngzhōu. They were trying to be a player on the world stage, but the foreign powers and big financial institutions all knew who buttered their bread in China and they continued to recognize the northern government based in Beijing for now. And like I said, you had Duàn and Féng in charge.

01:37 Duàn Qíruì represented the interests of the Wǎn Xì 皖系, the Ānhuī Clique. And Féng was the head of the Zhílì Clique, the Zhí Xì. Wǎn of course, for anyone who has ever seen an Ānhuī Province license plate knows, this is the one-character abbreviation of Ānhuī Province and all things Ānhuī.

02:00 Wǎn was one of those many small statelets that no one remembers from the Eastern Zhou times, more than 2,500 years ago.

02:11 A Xì was the Chinese term for clique or faction. In all the history books, these top warlord groups were referred to as cliques, which to me, going back to high school sort of always had a slightly negative connotation to it.

**02:29** Down in Guǎngzhōu, Sun Yat-sen and his followers didn't just lay down and die. They may not have had the international recognition they hoped for, but they still had their own powerful military backers. From 1917 to 1922 there was this warring period known as the Movement to Protect the Constitution, the Hùfǎ Yùndòng. The constitution being fought over was the provisional one that Yuan Shìkǎi had torn up in May 1914. Sun Yat-sen was leading the charge to restore that constitution written at the founding of the new nation. It was a civil war with on-again off-again battles.

**03:14** This Movement to Protect the Constitution also goes by another name. The KMT called it their Third Revolution. This war marks the start of hundreds of battles that would follow, big and small, of this warlord era. From the outset it was quite a mismatch.

**03:33** So down in the south, with a hundred former members of the National Assembly who opted to support the KMT rather than the northern warlords, they assembled and called for a Military Government to be established, based in Guǎngzhōu. And Sun Yat-sen was made the generalissimo or grand marshal, the Dà Yuán Shuài. Hey baby, that's a higher rank than field marshal and a five-star general. So, September 1, 1917 this parliament down in Guǎngzhōu…they created this new military government with the express intention of uniting the Chinese nation, challenging the Běiyáng generals, and making them toe the constitutional line.

**04:18** Easier said than done, as you'll see.

**04:20** I thought, for this episode, let's take a short break from all the headliners up in Beijing I've been mentioning and begin with the province of Húběi. If you're not familiar with Chinese geography, there are two neighboring provinces, Húběi to the north and Húnán to the south. This area, geographically, is as core central China as you can get. And not being on the coast and all, they don't get the attention that the coastal provinces have always enjoyed in popular modern Chinese history.

**04:55** And as we go along, you will see these two provinces were also quite central to the Warlord Era in China. Húběi-Húnán. They sort of played a geographic and strategic role as the buffer provinces separating the northern and southern governments of China. If you controlled Húnán, well, Guǎngdōng province was right next door and that was your convenient gateway to Guǎngzhōu where the KMT government was based.

**05:25** But let's step away from all these big names I've mentioned these past episodes and turn our attention to central China. In doing so I hope I can show you, in a microcosm, how things devolved so quickly and naturally into warlordism in China.

**05:43** The warlord down in Húběi was named Wáng Zhànyuán. I'm guessing most of you never heard of him. Unlike most warlords, he wasn't from the province where he made his mark in history. He came from a very poor background in rural Shāndōng. During the 1880s he got his start fighting as a soldier in Lǐ Hóngzhāng's Huái Army. You remember that from Part 1. They helped bring down the Tàipíngs.

06:10   Wáng Zhànyuán's big break came when he was admitted to the Tiānjìn Military Academy. Here he was able to shine and caught the attention of who else but Yuán Shìkǎi. And he was able to parlay this relationship with Yuán into a position in Yuan's New Army that later became the Běiyáng Army.

06:33   During the Second Revolution when the southern government attempted to organize a challenge to Yuan's authoritarianism, Wáng Zhànyuán, in what could later be said to have been a wise career move, stuck by Yuán Shìkǎi and assisted in putting this uprising down quickly.

06:50   Following a period of political maneuvering involving disparate interests in Húnán and Húběi, Yuán was able to install Wáng Zhànyuán as his guy down in Húběi province. This was in January of the fateful year of 1916. Well, fateful for Yuán Shìkǎi, that is.

07:11   This was the period when Yuán was making his grab for the emperorship. And he had placed all these loyal generals in all the governorships of all the provinces loyal to the Beiyang Clique. And he was counting on their support as soon as he became the Hóngxiàn Emperor.

07:31   However, following Yuán's failed bid to become emperor and March 1916 abdication not to mention the extreme diminishment in his prestige and political support, it was only a matter of time before his subordinates and their grand ambitions and ungovernable greed led them to turn their backs on their one-time benefactor. But as we know, Yuán Shìkǎi conveniently died in June 1916 and that was the primary accelerant that led to the warlord period.

**08:06** And what followed was a tragic parade lasting from 1916 to 1928 that saw twenty-six prime ministers, nine different presidents, a dysfunctional and hopelessly corrupt parliament and now these regional strongmen who took advantage of the times to withhold tax revenue, farm their provinces for treasure, obtain loans from foreign lenders and just line their pockets. And they thumbed their noses at any laws enacted by the central government in Beijing. And there was no central army controlled by the ROC government who could take these warlords on.

**08:50** And worst of all in the provinces where they ruled, they sucked the peasantry dry with every conceivable tax and regulation. Even in the poorest provinces in China, a warlord could make off like a bandit. So the peasantry, which back then was something like nine out of ten people walking around all the provinces of China, they bore the brunt of the worst of these famous excesses of these dūjūn or provincial military governors who called their own shots and weren't beholden to anyone in Beijing or Guǎngzhōu to prop them up.

**09:31** When Mao said in 1927 and 1938 — Qiānggǎnzi lǐmiàn chū zhèngquán: Political power grows out of the barrel of a gun—he must have been thinking about these warlords.

09:45 And all these smaller petty opportunistic militarists throughout the provinces, these mini warlords, they would swear allegiance to someone who swore allegiance to someone else and all the way up to the top of the pyramid to a particular provincial warlord serving as the military governor, the buck stopped with him as far as military and civil administration in the province.

10:09 The top warlords commanded a big army with lots of fire power and it was personally commanded by him. But it was the fealty from all these much smaller armies down at the grass roots level. That's how these major warlords controlled the province. And many, if not most of these petty minor warlords, they were nothing more than bandits, opportunists and predators of the worst kind.

10:39 And all throughout this warlord period, loyalty was not an everlasting commodity. These generals and all their officers down to the foot soldier switched sides and betrayed each other for whatever the uptick was in the market price for their loyalty. So the lines were always being redrawn according to the shifting allegiances among the various Cliques.

11:06 And Wáng Zhànyuán, he sort of led the pack. He was one of the first out of the starting gate you might say, who took advantage of the situation, Yuán Shìkǎi's demise. And all these Beiyang generals, they would either throw their lot in with Duàn Qíruì or they might choose Féng Guózhāng. Wáng Zhànyuán went with the Zhílì Clique which meant he took his marching orders from Féng Guózhāng.

**11:34**    Wáng Zhànyuán and many others like him during the second half of 1916, they were now spreading their wings and sharpening their claws as they began establishing personal control of their respective provinces. And no more was there one single strongman like Yuán Shìkǎi to inhibit them or boss them around.

**12:00**    From 1915 to 1921 Wáng Zhànyuán was in charge of all Húběi and ran it like a textbook warlord. He came down hard on his enemies and rivals. Despite all the initial violence, his early years were marked with general support from the masses and political leaders who appreciated the relative peace and order he had brought to Húběi. His soldiers were disciplined and he didn't carry out the kinds of violent acts that made these warlord soldiers so hated and despised. Chaos turned to order down in Húběi.

**12:41**    As long as order was present throughout Húběi, Wáng Zhànyuán remained firmly in charge. To preserve order it meant maintaining control over the troops under his command. He had already turned this 2nd Division of the Beiyang Army that Yuán Shìkǎi had given him command of into his personal army. All warlords did this. This became their core army and they just built on top of that.

**13:07**  In the beginning, Wáng Zhànyuán concerned himself only with military matters but in the wake of the Anti-Monarchical War, a.k.a. the Second Revolution, he expanded his control over civil affairs as well. As soon as he felt in control of things in Húběi, any loyalty Wáng Zhànyuán felt for his one-time benefactor Yuán Shìkǎi evaporated.

**13:34**  And Wáng Zhànyuán wasn't the only one I'm just using him as an example. Other warlords used the chaos that ensued during and after the Anti-Monarchical War to spread their tentacles throughout their respective provinces where Yuan had placed them. And through coercion and appointing officers and officials loyal to them, they assumed control over civil administration. Wáng Zhànyuán again, he was a nice textbook case of what I'm trying to present. Every province during the warlord era has their own history that sort of went this way.

**14:16**  With no opposition or viable opponents to stop him, Wáng Zhànyuán farmed every nickel he could harvest from Húběi province. In his day he was one of the richest men in China. He truly was one of the most predatory of all warlords, one of the extreme cases that gave these militarists their well-deserved bad reputation. During the years he controlled Húběi, he never missed an opportunity to maximize the amount of revenue that he could deposit into his personal bank account.

**14:53**  Besides the political and military events that were unfolding, Wáng Zhànyuán's undoing was his rapacious greed and the loss of popularity that happened with his own troops. From the most powerful warlord down to the basest soldier, everyone had their price. And time and again when one got cheap with their subordinates, immediately one's loyalties were put up for sale. And this is what Wáng Zhànyuán did. He got cheap with this troops, withheld pay, often for months, cheated on wages. And in an act that's all too familiar in today's business world, to cut costs, he tried to replace the older and more experienced soldiers with newer recruits who were willing to accept lower pay.

**15:44** This finally led to a series of mutinies in Hubei that led to violent civil disorder that led to loss of faith in Wáng as someone who could maintain order. And this ultimately led to Wáng Zhànyuán's undoing. That and of course other warlord actions such as printing too much money with denominations that ran in the millions. Never a good sign of a stable economy. He wasn't the last warlord to wear out a few printing presses. It got so bad with Wáng Zhànyuán that some officials in Wǔhàn were begging the foreigners to come in and establish control.

**16:26** There were two particularly violent and bloody mutinies by Wang's troops in the major cities of Yíchāng on June 4th, 1921 and Wǔchāng four days later. And these soldiers blew off a lot of steam about all the backpay that hadn't been paid and of course the attempt to marginalize all the over-forty soldiers in favor of younger, cheaper recruits. This created havoc and terror on the streets of those two cities and they got wrecked. By August 1921, Wáng Zhànyuán's fifteen minutes were up so to speak.

After he was toppled, he fled Húběi to Tiānjìn where he lived until 1934, dying at the age of seventy-four.

**17:16** By taking this little detour down to Húběi province and zeroing in on Wáng Zhànyuán, we can see that familiar pattern, how all this happened. Men like Wáng Zhànyuán didn't just appear out of nowhere. I've tried to show in Part 1 how the seed from which figures like Wáng Zhànyuán sprang forth was planted during the Taiping Rebellion and with the regional private armies who acted as the government's surrogates to quash national disturbances. In a desperate attempt to carry out a Great Leap Forward in China's military, academies such as those in Tiānjìn and Bǎodìng were being established that served as the incubators of future warlords and their associates.

**18:05** And we'll see moving forward Wáng Zhànyuán's story gets repeated all over China in every province. Wáng's story covered about six years,1915-1921. Lot's going on all over China. The May Fourth Movement and the founding of the CCP, the Chinese Communist Party. Let me just say the Warlords didn't like them. Communist Party members, organizers and outspoken supporters were always dodging the warlords. And the warlords, as you might guess, also weren't too keen on all the ideals of the May Fourth Movement, especially the ones about getting rid of the warlords.

**18:48** Let's go back and talk about the setup for one of the main headlining events of the early Warlord Era. This was the Zhílì-Ānhuī War. It was only a matter of time before these militarists all started turning on each other. Summer of 1917 there had been a big confrontation down in Húnán. This province next door to Húběi had declared independence and Duàn Qíruì was itching to take his army down there and bang some heads. He needed Húnán on his side rather than having the Húnán Army lean towards Sun Yat-sen.

19:30 But Féng Guózhāng was staying Duàn's hand and saying, don't start a war. Let's negotiate a settlement with respect to Húnán and this whole Constitutional Protection War.

19:43 The two most powerful forces in China, Duàn Qíruì and Féng Guózhāng, had been at loggerheads over every single hot button issue since Yuan's death. But with regard to the situation down in the key province of Húnán, matters finally came to a head. Duàn viewed Húnán as his short cut into the neighboring rival provinces of Guǎngdōng and Guǎngxī. When Húnán trended towards the Beiyang government things were fine. But by declaring independence, that became a serious impediment to Duàn's unification plans in China, with him on top.

20:26 Duàn Qíruì pushed Feng aside and indicated he wasn't in a negotiating mood and he sent his Ānhuī forces down south to drag the Húnán government back into the Běiyáng fold.

20:41 In short, Duàn's army was soundly defeated by the combined forces from Yunnan, Guǎngxī and Húnán.

By November 1917 Duàn Qíruì's armies, after a poor showing, had to throw in the towel. And following this defeat on the battlefield, the beleaguered Duàn Qíruì had to resign as premier. For now, the fighting ceased. But the problems remained.

21:08 In the meantime over in Russia, the Bolshevik Revolution happened. This is going to have a rather profound impact on China in the years to come.

21:20 As 1918 dawned the Féng Guózhāng allies Wú Pèifú and Cáo Kūn led Zhílì Clique forces down to Húnán and defeated the army down there. That was in April 1918. This was followed by a negotiated peaceful settlement with Guǎngdōng and Guǎngxī representatives spearheaded by Wú Pèifú. The situation wasn't resolved, but things quieted down on the fields of battle.

21:52 Féng Guózhāng, leader of the Zhílì Clique, he began to have health issues around the time his five-year term as president ended in 1918. And by the end of 1919 he passed away, handing the reigns of power to the Běiyáng stalwart and loyal Zhílì Clique general Cáo Kūn.

22:13 The presidency of the Republic was passed to a long-time Yuán Shìkǎi comrade, Xú Shìchāng. They were of the same generation and Xú was a few years Yuan's senior. He was a nice compromise candidate, not military, Běiyáng friendly but allied to neither the Ānhuī nor the Zhílì Clique.

22:36 | Those of you who remember the Peter O'Toole character in the Last Emperor? It was Xú Shìchāng who had been the Chinese leader who arranged for Reginald Johnston to tutor the former emperor Pǔyí.

22:50 | Anyway, he was on duty as president of the Republic of China from Oct 10, 1918 to June 2, 1922. That means he was president during the events that led up to, during and after May Fourth, that epochal movement in modern Chinese history in 1919.

23:37 | Let me just prime the pump for Part 5 in this series by introducing a couple names I've just mentioned. Two biggies. Cáo Kūn and Wú Pèifú. Some names in this warlord saga are bigger than others. So as we proceed up and down along the timeline, I'm going to occasionally pull off to the shoulder and briefly introduce the backgrounds of the more important figures and where they fit into our story.

23:54 | And these two, they were pretty big. Cáo Kūn, the one who picked up where Féng Guózhāng left off as head of the Zhílì Clique, he was just a few years younger than Yuán Shìkǎi and they had risen together in the Běiyáng organization.

24:15 | Cáo came from near Tiānjìn, Zhílì country. He came from nothing and in an oft-repeated story I'm sure you're gonna get tired of hearing, he rose up through the ranks of the Běiyáng Army, eventually commanding his own division. So he was a very high-up general in the Běiyáng military.

Bad blood existed between Cáo Kūn and Duàn Qíruì. This went back to Duàn's role in thwarting Cáo Kūn's aspirations to the vice-presidency of the Republic. The political wing of the Ānhuī Clique was known as the Ānfú Club. They bought their way into the National Assembly and did Duàn Qíruì's bidding in political and government affairs.

24:41 There are a number of battles and political maneuverings that Cáo Kūn was involved in but in popular Chinese history he's best remembered as the guy who brazenly bribed his way to the presidency of the republic. Cáo was a politician at heart even though fate made him a warlord. While he dabbled in the politics of the northern China government, the official one recognized by the foreign powers, he left all the military heavy lifting to his number two, Wú Pèifú. Cáo Kūn, if you can say nothing else about him, wanted to be president of China.

25:22 So he used his warlord wealth and influence and bought his way into that top spot. The popular anecdote that has been passed down since the moment it happened was that supposedly he was handing out five thousand silver dollars to any National Assemblyman who would give him his vote.

25:41 It was done out in the open. No attempt was made to try and hide it, and when he became the sixth president in 1923-1924, everyone knew how he got there and despite the corruptible times they lived in, everyone around him sort of held their nose and shunned Cáo Kūn.

**26:03** By the start of the 1920s, the warlords were already acquiring a very smelly and odious reputation amongst the people, and certainly amongst the intelligentsia who couldn't write enough bad things about Cáo. And the ill-will didn't stop at Cáo Kūn. By extension the entire Běiyáng military organization, because of Cáo's blatant corruption, took a hit to their share price. That's all in the future, however. We're still in 1919.

**26:33** Cáo's closest comrade in the Zhílì Clique of the Běiyáng organization, as I said, was Wú Pèifú. He was one of the major stars of the Warlord Saga, a very influential and historic figure. Made the cover of Time Magazine in September 1924. I'm not going to say he didn't play a role in keeping China weak and divided in his capacity as a militarist, but he's generally regarded as one of the more acceptable faces of warlordism.

**27:08** Wú Pèifú was very educated. Born in Pénglái, Shāndōng province. Same hometown as Qī Jìguāng who we featured not too long ago in CHP-230. He passed all the imperial exams and was a very cultured and educated guy. But despite all that background and education, Wú Pèifú turned his back on the civil bureaucracy and elected instead to enter the military. And if I told you he graduated from the Bǎodìng Military Academy and later served in Yuán Shìkǎi's New Army I suppose you'd have no reason not to believe me. So he had his own command in the Běiyáng Army and like everyone in that organization he, too, took sides. He went with Team Zhílì.

**27:57** Though he came from Shāndōng, Wú Pèifú's power base was in Hénán, central China, in the ancient eastern capital of Luòyáng. Not exactly Zhílì country, but he had taken Féng Guózhāng's side when the Běiyáng Clique began to splinter. Cáo Kūn assumed the place of leadership in the Zhílì Clique and Cáo had Wú Pèifú and one other warlord we will get to next episode, Sūn Chuánfāng, these two, as his right and left hands.

**28:28** And as we close out this Part 4 episode we see a civil war quietly percolating within the northern Beiyang Clique. Cáo Kūn and Wú Pèifú, in their determination to bring down Duàn Qíruì and expose him as a traitor to China and a stooge of Japan, went to great lengths to publicly smear Duàn in the press and in various other circles of power and influence.

**28:57** So as the battle lines were being drawn between Duàn Qíruì's Ānhuī Clique and Cáo Kūn's Zhílì Clique, both sides got ready for the inevitable showdown. This is what we'll look at next time. The first Zhílì-Ānhuī War. You won't want to miss that. Next episode, I promise you we'll finally get to the Old Marshal, the Manchurian Warlord, Zhāng Zuòlín. He's gonna get a little spooked at Duàn Qíruì's actions and will line up behind Cáo Kūn and Wú Pèifú in the upcoming war.

**29:31** Thank you everyone if you made it this far. This is still Laszlo Montgomery signing off from the city that made Southern California famous, Los Angeles, the Big Orange.

THE WARLORD ERA
PART 4

THE
CHP
CHINA HISTORY PODCAST
THE TRANSCRIPTS

**29:42** OK, that's all for now. Do consider joining me again next time for another hearty and filling episode of the China History Podcast.

 The Warlord Era
Part 5

## SUMMARY

In Part 5 Laszlo gives the backstory to the Anhui-Zhili War and introduces another warlord, the famous "Manchurian Warlord," Zhang Zuolin. With the civil war within the Beiyang Organization, the unity that existed since the time of Yuan Shikai is smashed. We'll look at the very brief war between the forces of Duan Qirui and their Zhili opponents led by Wu Peifu as well as the aftermath up to and including the First Zhili-Fengtian War, 1922-1924.

## TRANSCRIPT

00:00 | Welcome back everyone, Laszlo Montgomery here, bringing you China History Podcast episode 235. Part 5 in our overview of the Chinese Warlord Era that lasted 1916 to 1928. And still lingered on after that but let's not get too far ahead of ourselves.

00:21 | Last time in Part 4, I left you hanging right at the lead-up to the first Ānhuī-Zhílì War. They should have called it the Ānhuī-Zhílì Battle. It only lasted nine days. From here on out, there will be a number of these military clashes amongst the various cliques. As we keep walking along the timeline, I'll introduce them to you one at a time. This Ānhuī-Zhílì War was the first.

00:52 Last time in Part 4, we saw how in late 1917 Duàn Qíruì and his forces had gone down into Húnán to put an end to this breakaway province's ambitions of independence from the northern Běiyáng Clique-dominated government. But after a poor showing and failing in the main mission, Duàn had to go back to Beijing with his tail between his legs. He shortly thereafter resigned from the premiership and withdrew from the scene to lick his wounds and ponder the seething ill feelings he had for Féng Guózhāng, Cáo Kūn and Wú Pèifú, the Big Three of the Zhílì Clique.

01:36 And not just that, at the time of this Ānhuī-Zhílì War Duàn was really catching a ton of grief about the terms of those Nishihara loans. That whole transaction, as beneficial as it was to the Ānhuī Clique organization, had done nothing to help his brand. The Mukden Incident where Japan really lets it all hang out, was still thirteen years away. But by accepting that 150 or 200 million yen loan, Duàn Qíruì really rolled out the red carpet for the Japanese in northern China.

02:15 And not just that. You know how, back in the Hàn Dynasty, we always associate the word "usurper" with the statesman and later emperor Wáng Mǎng. Well, for Duàn Qíruì the word "traitor" ended up getting indelibly attached to his name. He caught a lot of grief, as did a lot of others who got too friendly with the Japanese around this time.

02:40 By April 1918, Cáo Kūn had sent forces down to Húnán and accomplished what Duàn could not. The

Constitutional Protection Army, the Hùfǎjūn was pushed out. And then after settling scores in Húnán, the Zhílì Clique, resisting Duàn's continued insistence on a military solution to defeat the southern renegade provinces, well, rather than take the fight this far south, Wú Pèifú became the man of the hour by negotiating a peaceful settlement with the three biggest warlords down there. And we'll get to them later on.

**03:18** These were Táng Jìyáo in Yúnnán, Lù Róngtíng in Guǎngxī and Chén Jiǒngmíng in Guǎngdōng. After everyone was able to come to an agreement, that ratcheted things down a few notches between the rival northern and southern governments. And that also spelled the end of the Constitutional Protection War.

**03:41** In May of 1918, the southern government led by Sun Yat-sen was re-organized and all the decision-making spots were filled with military men.

**03:53** I have nothing against the military, but filling all the top government ministries, governorships and executive branch positions with these fellas in charge was no way to launch a republic.

**04:06** And as WWI comes to an end, China is all carved up mainly between the southern government led by Sun Yat-sen and his military backers and the much larger but fractured northern government. And where there used to be one single voice, Yuán Shìkǎi's, who spoke for the north, now we have multiple contenders. Duàn Qíruì and the Ānhuī Clique and their military assets were now in a wrestling match with the Zhílì Clique that, up until his death at the end of 1919, was led by Féng Guózhāng. And as Féng's health had begun to fade, the mantle of leadership of the Zhílì Clique was passed to Cáo Kūn. And Cáo's two deputies were Wú Pèifú and Sūn Chuánfāng. Cáo and Wú we looked at briefly last episode. I'll get to Sūn Chuánfāng in Part 6 or 7. These are all top names from this warlord era.

05:07    Cáo Kūn had a passion for being a player in the political arena. His right hand man Wú Pèifú, was more the military expert. So they were a team.

05:18    Before we dive into the Ānhuī-Zhílì War, let me first introduce another major warlord of this time. This was Zhāng Zuòlín. Of all the warlords I'll introduce, he managed to hang onto power the longest. He was at the head of the Fèngtiān Clique out in the northeast, Manchuria. One more for you to remember.

05:41    For the twenty-two years lasting from 1907 to 1929, when all this is taking place, Liáoníng province was known as Fèngtiān province.

05:54    Zhāng Zuòlín ran Manchuria, today's provinces of Hēilóngjiāng, Jílín and Liáoníng. He had his own set of nicknames, but the Manchurian Warlord was what he gets called most often, I would venture to say. With The Tiger of Manchuria in second place. The Old Marshal, he's also known as, to differentiate him from his son Zhāng Xuéliáng, known as The Young Marshal, way way in the future.

06:24 | Zhāng Zuòlín was born in Hǎichéng, a city about midway between Shěnyáng and Dàlián, Liáoníng Province. He was the third son of a poor family and only had about two years of any kind of formal schooling. Unlike his future adversary Wú Pèifú, he was not an educated man. According to one of the legends from his youth, he tried to avenge his father's death, and in carrying out the act, he used a little too much force and had to flee his hometown.

06:58 | With limited options, Zhāng Zuòlín joined the army and saw action in the Sino-Japanese War. After that, he ended up taking a position as a kind of security guard for his father-in-law's village. In these times, roving bandit gangs were endemic all over northern China. They would march into any number of quiet little villages and just plunder the hell out of them, turn 'em upside down, conscript a male or two and move on to their next meal. Villages and towns that could afford it, would recruit a small militia to protect them from this early 20th century scourge.

07:41 | They had a name for these security guards or roving militias. They called them Red Beards, Hóng Húzi.

07:48 | Zhāng Zuòlín had the good fortune to end up in the right place at the right time on a number of occasions. He and a couple others who became part of his inner circle, rose up to positions of power fighting against these bandits at the provincial level. He also stood by the Qing government's side during the Boxer Rebellion.

08:09 And during the Russo-Japanese War, he fought on Japan's side and used his army to harass the Russians. And as far as Zhāng Zuòlín's association with the Japanese, that support he gave Japan during that war ended up being the beginning of a beautiful relationship, for a while.

08:31 By 1907 after folding his troops into the provincial army, Zhāng Zuòlín was commanding his own battalion. At the time of the Wǔchāng Uprising, 1911, at the behest of the governor general, he put down the revolutionary forces there and helped keep Shěnyáng and all of Liáoníng loyal to the emperor, at least until a better offer came.

08:56 Upon the establishment of the Republic of China, Zhāng Zuòlín ended up getting in real tight with Yuán Shìkǎi and by now, had the command of his own division. And these forces became the core of his military power. I said that last episode. The command given to these Běiyáng generals by Yuán Shìkǎi, their rank and the troops that came with that rank served as their elite personal army later on.

09:26 In return for backing Yuán in his run for the emperorship, Zhang was made governor-general of Fèngtiān. And really, as I said before with Wáng Zhànyuán in Húběi, that's all you needed. That was the golden ticket you had to hold in order to become a warlord. In this way not only did Zhāng Zuòlín command the military, but he had his hands on the controls of the civilian government as well.

**09:54** And after Yuán died and that free-for-all happened when every governor-general began to transform into a warlord in their respective provinces, Zhāng Zuòlín was no exception. He kicked out the governors-general of the other two provinces and filled those spots with his own nominees. And by doing so, he took over all three provinces that made up Manchuria. These two other military governors, these dūjūn's put in place by Zhāng, they were able to run their respective provinces like any other warlord, but always deferred to Zhāng Zuòlín in all matters that he got involved in.

**10:34** Remember when all this happened, Duàn Qíruì had taken over from Yuán Shìkǎi and in order to consolidate his power he needed to make a lot of friends. So he won Zhāng Zuòlín over to his side by appointing him Inspector-General of the Eastern Three Provinces. And once he got comfortable there in those Eastern Three Provinces of Manchuria, Zhāng Zuòlín continued to put together his own power base that included local military officers and other elites of the realm. And as I said, this became known as the Fèngtiān Clique. The Ānhuī and Zhílì Cliques will try to win him over to their side. But Zhāng always looked out for number one first and always.

**11:22** And he ran these three provinces of northeast China with as iron a fist as any warlord. He had to constantly fight off attempts by the central government to dilute his control of Manchuria by sending all these appointees in his direction. Zhang was very adept at keeping the central government at bay and controlling all of Manchuria by himself. And even though it was technically part of the Republic of China, he negotiated directly with foreign powers, signed treaties, cut deals… Everyone who had an ounce of political astuteness knew Zhang Zuolin was the ultimate authority in that northeast corner of China.

12:06　Anyway, later on after he had consolidated all his power in Manchuria, his attention turned southward, in the direction of northern China. And this ambition he had to take Beijing for himself would end up conflicting with the interests of Cáo Kūn and Wú Pèifú. But for now, the enemy of my enemy is my friend. and in this war that was brewing, Zhāng Zuòlín took the side of the Zhílì Clique against Duàn Qíruì and his Ānhuī Clique armies.

12:40　Zhílì, Ānhuī and now Fèngtiān. These three warlord groups all contending in the north. And remember, whoever controlled Beijing, that was the official government of China that world leaders and diplomats dealt with, not to mention the bankers as well. And because the northern government was so fractured and unable to agree on anything, we remember China, in 1919 got taken to the cleaners at the Treaty of Versailles.

13:10　So this Manchurian Warlord, he was quite good at building bonds between himself and his key military allies.

13:18　And it didn't stop there. The Zhílì-Fèngtiān alliance also sought to build strategic bridges with southern warlords in Guǎngxī and Yúnnán. And as the drumbeat got louder, other warlords in central and eastern China will line up with Cáo Kūn and Wú Pèifú against Duàn Qíruì in this Ānhuī-Zhílì War.

13:44 This had all been brewing for a while. What really started up the gears of war involved a political crisis that followed Duàn Qíruì's incursions into Outer Mongolia. He had sent one of his top generals there to take back Outer Mongolia for the Republic of China. As I said, Zhāng Zuòlín didn't like that. Having Anhui Clique forces this close to Manchuria was too close for comfort. And for sure, the Zhílì faction wasn't happy. So after one of Duan's right hand men Xú Shùzhēng took his armies into Mongolia, the Fèngtiān and Zhílì Cliques ended up becoming strange bedfellows for this war against Duàn's Anhui Forces.

14:31 Xú Shùzhēng was the de facto leader of the Ānfú Club and a very close comrade of Duan Qirui. Remember them from last episode? The Ānfú Club, because it was located out of Ānfú Lane in Beijing. This was the political arm of Duàn Qíruì's whole Ānhuī organization. They dominated the Běijīng government.

14:55 Xú got yanked out of Mongolia by the compromise president, who I mentioned last time, someone having the confusingly similar name of Xú Shìchāng. Two Xú's but they ain't on the same side.

15:09 Being challenged so blatantly like this, Duàn had no choice but to pull Xú Shùzhēng's army out of Mongolia and get them heading in a southerly direction, towards Běijīng to take on their Zhílì enemies. Duan and Xú

**THE WARLORD ERA**
PART 5

THE
**CHP**
CHINA HISTORY PODCAST
**THE TRANSCRIPTS**

Shùzhēng of the Ānhuī Clique versus the combined forces of the Zhílì and Fèngtiān cliques. And the prize was control of the Beiyang organization that operated all the buttons and levers of the northern government based in Beijing.

15:42    Bad blood had arose between these two opposing factions ever since the Hùfǎ Yùndòng, the Constitutional Protection Movement. With everyone now in control of their own armies and with so much at stake in this post WWI period in China, the battles began.

15:59    Towards the end of 1919, Wú Pèifú had already cemented alliances between his Zhílì clique and Táng Jìyáo of the Yunnan Clique and Lù Róngtíng of the Guǎngxī clique. And they, as well as other warlords in central and northern China all ganged up on Duàn Qíruì and his Ānhuī clique. And to light this powder keg, the shot across the bow that sparked this Ānhuī-Zhílì War, this first open warfare between the once unified Beiyang warlords, was the open denouncement of Duàn Qíruì signed by all of Wú Pèifú's warlord allies. No words were minced and Duan was called out for his traitorous deeds, primarily with respect to the Nishihara loans.

16:51    So, between being dissed by having his guy pulled out of Outer Mongolia and all the drubbing he was getting in the media from stories planted by Zhílì clique leaders, he had to respond.

17:04    And, like I said at the outset, this war didn't last terribly long. It took place about fifty miles south of

Beijing. The Ānhuī armies led by Duàn, Xú Shùzhēng and Qǔ Tóngfēng went on the offensive and had a few good days until Wú Pèifú's armies turned everything around. July 17, we're in the year 1920, Wú Pèifú's troops overwhelmed the Ānhuī armies and captured the general Qǔ Tóngfēng.

17:36 And Zhāng Zuòlín was holding down the fort two hundred fifty miles to the east, right where the Great Wall meets the Bóhǎi Sea. As soon as things took a turn for the worse for the Ānhuī forces, Zhāng Zuòlín's Fèngtiān army attacked from the east and everything fell apart for Duàn Qíruì. With so much firepower from all directions lined up against him, the odds weren't good to begin with. But with Zhāng Zuòlín moving in hard and fast from the east, it ended quickly.

18:08 And with Duàn Qíruì on the run, the victorious Zhílì and Fèngtiān Cliques took over the reins of power in the Běijīng government. Whatever unity that once existed in the Běiyáng organization, those days were now over. So July 1920, there's a new team in control of the northern government. Duàn Qíruì had run it since Yuán Shìkǎi died in June 1916. Xú Shìchāng remained the president of the Republic, serving till June 1922.

18:44 Duàn Qíruì with this defeat was no longer an important player and from now on he stays in the backseat until he's dragged back into the government from 1924 to 1926 as a compromise Chief Executive of the Republic. We'll get to that in Part 6 or 7. Until then, Duàn kept a low profile living inside the Japanese settlement in

Tiānjīn and later in Shanghai. In his retirement he had become an extremely devout Buddhist and found solace in the religion until his death in November 1936. In 1920, the Ānhuī Clique, well, it didn't disappear, but it sort of dissolved. And most of the officers and politicians either went in the direction of Fèngtiān or Zhílì.

**19:35** This was quite a victory for Zhāng Zuòlín. Wú Pèifú's armies had done all the heavy lifting in defeating the Ānhuī army. Zhāng Zuòlín's troops did more mopping up than anything. But like I said, he was good at capitalizing on whatever opportunities came his way.

**19:53** So these two victorious factions, Zhāng Zuòlín's Fèngtiān Clique and Wú Pèifú and Cao Kun's Zhílì Clique, they formed a coalition government. And quotation marks around that word "coalition." And in less than two years the Manchurian Warlord and the Jade Marshal, Wu Peifu, will be at each other's throats.

**20:18** And right as this Zhílì Ānhuī War ends, there's a terrible famine in north China. Most affected were the people of Zhílì, Shāndōng, Shānxī, Shǎnxī and Hénán. This was known as the Great North China Famine of the winter of 1920-21. Thanks to incredible humanitarian efforts, only half a million peasants perished in this natural disaster. But there were other famines and natural disasters around China that happened during these years at the dawn of the 1920's. Warlordism wasn't the direct cause of these famines but it was additional layer of misery added on top of the breakdown in law and order and how that affected the peasantry in their daily lives.

**21:09** Anyway, up in Beijing, as I indicated, cordial relations between Wú Pèifú and Zhāng Zuòlín in no time at all were starting to break down. Zhāng Zuòlín, he had a lot of ambition and was very much intent on squeezing out Wú Pèifú, seizing sole control of the government, and then, unify China by defeating the southern warlords, a similar dream like Xiàng Yǔ and Liú Bāng once had, going back over twenty-one centuries before.

**21:44** And Wu Peifu, he had the same idea. So you know where this was heading. Whoever controlled the historic and symbolic city of Beijing was, in the eyes of those inside and outside China, the legitimate government of the country. And Beijing was only big enough for one warlord. And one of them had to go.

**22:08** And it ran deeper than this, wheels within wheels. The Western nations with a finger in China's pie, they mostly lined up behind Wu Peifu. And as I mentioned, even though he was no less a patriot than any other leader, Zhang Zuolin had Japan watching his back.

**22:27** With this competition between the two warlord cliques, it was only a matter of time before something would ignite the powder keg. Zhang Zuolin went and did a sneaky thing. He installed one of his men, Liáng Shìyí, as premier. A very bold power move that would have given Zhang control of the government through the office of premier. We've mentioned Liáng Shìyí before in previous episodes. He was one of Yuan Shikai's political cronies going way back.

**22:57** As soon as Wu Peifu found out what Zhang Zuolin had gone and done, his outrage was predictable. And after Liáng Shìyí started holding up government funds that should have gone in the direction of the Zhili Clique, that was it. Decisions were being made in Beijing independent of Wú Pèifú which made a mockery of the whole idea of a coalition government. Liáng Shìyí was forced by Wu Peifu to resign after a month. And then these two sides geared up for battle.

**23:31** Like the Zhílì Ānhuī War, this one, known as the First Zhílì-Fèngtiān War, was quick too. April, May and June 1922. Where was it fought? Same as before, south of Beijing and Tiānjìn.

**23:48** Over the course of the fighting, Zhāng Zuòlín's forces appeared to have this one in the bag. He attacked on two fronts from the east and west. At first he pushed Wu Peifu's armies back on their heels. But for the second time, as he had done against the Ānhuī forces, Wu Peifu outsmarted, outflanked and outperformed his opponent's main army and pushed them all the way to the China coast, to Shānhǎiguān.

**24:18** Wú Pèifú, he had a little help from former Zhili troops who had defected to Zhang Zuolin's side after the death of Feng Guozhang in 1919 and then rejoined Zhili forces after the outbreak of this war.

**24:34** Let me tell you they won't be the first army to switch sides in the middle of a war and change the tide of battle. Finally the British had to be called in to broker a peace.

As part of the deal, Zhang Zuolin had to remove his army from south of Shānhǎiguān, over near Qínhuángdǎo in Héběi Province, still called Zhili province as all this is happening. Zhang's armies suffered seventy thousand killed, wounded or captured. And in these times, desertion was also rampant. He had to start rebuilding at once. Either way you look at it, the First Zhili Fèngtiān War was a bitter defeat for Zhang Zuolin.

25:22   And once Zhāng Zuòlín was safely back in Manchuria after suffering this defeat on the military and political battlefield, Wú Pèifú and the Zhílì Clique scraped away all remnant Fèngtiān Clique men out of any position of power in Beijing. And now they ran it for themselves.

25:44   And with the Fèngtiān Clique no longer in positions of power in Beijing, the Japanese weren't happy about the outcome either. With Wu Peifu, a well-known Japan hater in charge, things weren't going to be as easy for them in north China.

25:59   And here is where Wú Pèifú, over the next two years, rose to become the most powerful and prominent leader in northern and central China. Zhāng Zuòlín continued to tightly control Manchuria. No one could challenge him on his home turf. He had declared autonomy in Manchuria and stood a Band Apart from the Beijing government now dominated by Wu Peifu and the Zhili politicians and militarists.

26:29   In all the provinces of the north all the way down to Hunan, Wú Pèifú to varying degrees controlled what went on there. And as I said in September 1924, Time Magazine had him on their cover.

26:45 And not more than two weeks after Wu Peifu made the cover of Time, he and Zhang Zuolin were at it again in the Second Zhili-Fèngtiān War. I'm not going to get into that here. We'll save that for next time.

26:58 Listening to these past episodes, you'd almost think these wars were all that was going on in China. Well, that was hardly the case. With no one single emperor or king or party chairman in charge of the whole country, there were sideshows going on all over the place. In Xinjiang. In Tibet. In Guangzhou and Hong Kong, Guangxi, all of those southern provinces. Shanghai in the 1920s, we've looked at from all kinds of angles. That whole world that evokes a thousand images in culture, entertainment and commerce. That too was all happening during these warlord years.

27:43 Well, the list of warlords is getting longer and longer and these were just the major ones. In the First Zhili Fèngtiān War, it was more than Zhang Zuolin and Wu Peifu commanding troops. I'm going out of my way to spare you from too many names raining down on you.

28:04 We'll pickup in Part 6 with the continuation of this story and the lead up to the Second Zhili-Fèngtiān War. I'll give you a hint. This one turns out a little better for the Manchurian Warlord.

**28:17** And how can we talk about the Second Zhili-Fèngtiān War without introducing Féng Yùxiáng, The Christian Warlord? He's a favorite of many, another colorful character from this miserable time.

**28:31** Even in our day on all our news feeds and on TV, we can see cities and countries around the world that are wracked with civil war, political division and human suffering. This kind of thing is as old as history itself. And in the 1920s, it was China's turn to be the one hit with this instability. And like it is everywhere, the peasants and common people trying to survive the times inevitably suffered the greatest.

**29:06** I don't want you to lose hope. These warlords, they do finally get neutralized. We'll get to that happy ending, I assure you.

**29:14** Okay, that's it for now everyone. Laszlo Montgomery here signing off from Los Angeles California on a gorgeous November day. I had to turn on my A/C today it was so hot. Think about coming back again, once more with feeling, for Part 6 in our ever-expanding warlord series here at the China History Podcast.

# THE CHP
**CHINA HISTORY PODCAST**
**THE TRANSCRIPTS**

## The Warlord Era
## Part 6

## SUMMARY

Things were looking on the up and up for Wu Peifu after his defeat of Zhang Zuolin in the First Zhili-Fengtian War. In this episode, we look at the years 1922-24 and the Second Zhili-Fengtian War. And you can't talk about the Second Zhiuli-Fengtian War without also mentioning the Jiangsu-Zhejiang War. The Christian Warlord Feng Yuxiang is featured in this episode. Besides the old stalwarts, also mentioned in this episode will be Lu Yongxiang, Qi Xieyuan, Sun Chuanfang, and Zhang Zongchang.

## TRANSCRIPT

00:00 | Welcome back again, everyone. Laszlo Montgomery here bringing you Part 6 in this series where we're giving the Warlord Era in China a once-over. This slice of Republican era history lasted from Yuán Shìkǎi's death in 1916 until the end of the Northern Expedition that we haven't gotten to yet but will one day, but not in this episode.

00:25 | We left off in Part 5 in 1922 with Wú Pèifú riding high in the saddle as the undisputed power in Běijīng where the official government of the Republic of China was located. He had just won an overwhelming victory over Zhāng Zuòlín's forces in the First Zhílì-Fèngtiān War.

00:47 While all this is happening in the north, there's a whole parallel universe happening down in the south that we've only touched on here and there. Our focus thus far in this series has mostly been with respect to what was happening up north with the Běiyáng government rather than the rival government led by Sun Yat-sen in Canton, Guangzhou.

01:08 With Wú Pèifú in charge in Beijing, one of the first things he tried to establish was a good government that could lead from the top down. He assembled what became known as the Cabinet of Able Men. The call had gone out for all men of talent to come forth and serve their country at this hour of need. You may recall from that Wellington Koo episode, he was one of those patriotic Chinese who left his idyllic life as an overseas diplomat to become part of this cabinet that Wú Pèifú was personally putting together.

01:43 Prior to that, Wú Pèifú had re-established the parliament. That august body hadn't had a legitimate meeting since 1917. And they dusted off Lí Yuánhóng too and brought him back as the new president of the Republic, the only one to serve twice in this position, which in a way makes him the Grover Cleveland of modern China. They both had mustaches too.

02:07 You'd think, at last, this could be the break the Chinese nation needed. After all, Wú Pèifú, besides being called The Jade Marshal, he was also referred to as the Philosopher Warlord or General, because he was so educated, cultured and had passed all the old civil service exams in his younger days. Sure, there was that little military dictatorship thing. But aside from that, there was this brief moment where it was thought under his leadership and military strength to back it up, this might work out.

02:42   But it didn't. By November 1922 within the Zhílì Clique itself there was an open split between the two most powerful heads. That is, Cáo Kūn and Wú Pèifú. Though Cáo was the figurehead as far as the head of the Zhílì Clique went, it was generally acknowledged by all that it was Wú Pèifú who wore the trousers in the family, and this led to Cáo going to extraordinary lengths to make himself more than just a figurehead.

03:14   This was the time, you may recall from Part 4 when I first introduced Cáo Kūn, this was when he was buying his way into the presidency, paying five thousand dollars bribes to anyone in the provisional assembly who gave him their vote. He got to be the sixth president of the ROC, serving from October 10, 1923 to November 2, 1924.

03:38   Not that he was a paragon of virtue, but Wú Pèifú wasn't happy about the way Cáo Kūn had gone and done what he did. There was a lot of blowback from the public and Wú Pèifú had to answer to all the national outrage about Cáo taking corruption to a whole new level.

03:57   With all this discord between Cáo Kūn and Wú Pèifú, there went the Jade Marshal's whole big idea. From the top down, the cabinet, the parliament, poor Lí Yuánhóng, all these so-called "Able Men" like Wellington Koo and Wáng Chǒnghuì, who, given better circumstances, might have been able to make a difference. Without the essential unity within the Zhílì Clique top leadership, this whole thing fizzled out quite quickly.

04:30 And by 1924 there came another in a long line of showdowns between rival warlords. Let's get started with the backstory to this Second Zhílì Fèngtiān War and along the way I'll introduce a few more warlords who join the fray.

04:48 Zhāng Zuòlín, after he was defeated by Wú Pèifú on the battlefield, went back to his stronghold in Manchuria and embarked on a very serious military modernization plan and spared no expense to obtain the best military hardware that his formidable resources could afford. Now that aviation was far enough advanced, Zhāng Zuòlín built an air force from the ground up and put his son Zhāng Xuéliáng, the Young Marshal, in charge of this.

05:19 And he trained his forces to no end and aggressively prepared for the showdown that was surely to come. Either he went out and got rid of Wú Pèifú or it was gonna be the other way around. Zhāng Zuòlín had bigger ambitions than being the Manchurian Warlord. And Zhāng Zuòlín's Japanese supporters, who were placing all their chips on him, they were only too willing to lend a hand or grease the wheels if called upon to help out in the effort of getting rid of Wú Pèifú.

**05:52** Like last time, before these two giants, Zhāng Zuòlín and Wú Pèifú, before they took the fight to the other they both went out and started shopping for alliances. Despite their defeat in the Ānhuī-Zhílì War, Duàn Qíruì and the Ānhuī Clique were still around. They might not have had the power they once had in 1917, but they still had some influence. Their last stronghold was in Shandong province and they had influence elsewhere. They decided to cozy up to Zhāng Zuòlín and give their support to his Fèngtiān Clique.

**06:03** Zhāng Zuòlín also approached the KMT down in Guǎngzhōu and tried to win them over. Some interesting things were happening inside the KMT at this moment. I'm going to focus on this in a bit, or maybe next episode.

**06:46** By the way, January 26, 1923 came the Sun-Joffe Joint Statement. Sun Yat-sen, for lack of anyone else interested in supporting him and his KMT, joined hands with Adolf Joffe from the Comintern. The USSR had been formally established on December 30, 1922. The Soviets had big plans for China. And as an opening gambit in this soon to be messy and complicated political situation, Joffe, on behalf of the Comintern, swore to support Sun Yat-sen in his efforts to unify the country. And they had a plan.

**07:27** Later in June 1924 over at the new Whampoa Military Academy, a thirty-seven-year-old Chiang Kai-shek was made the top guy there. That fine institution was built with Soviet money and run on a similar model as you'd find in the Soviet Union. Sun Yat-sen was nominally in charge of everything and based in Guǎngzhōu, serving

THE
CHP
CHINA HISTORY PODCAST
THE TRANSCRIPTS

THE WARLORD ERA
PART 6

as the generalissimo or grand marshal of this southern military government, whose ultimate mission again, was to unify the country.

08:00 So this ill-fated experiment between the Guómíndǎng and the Soviets was giving itself a dry run. This is where Chiang Kai-shek enters the story but let's hold off before we start talking about him.

08:12 And to make this happen the Soviet advisors down in the south of China, dragged the Communists and Nationalists into a First United Front where the two sides would join together in the common objective of bringing down all the warlords and unifying China. This was the first time these two sides came together. We all know over the next two and a half decades... but we all know how that's gonna work out ultimately.

08:39 And if you recall from that Zhōu Ēnlái eight-part series, Zhōu was the one who ended up in Guǎngzhōu in September 1924 as the CCP representative serving in the Political Department of the Whampoa Military Academy.

08:53 And in July 1926 when Chiang launched the Northern Expedition, it will be from here, at Whampoa where he will lead his army north. All coming up later in this series.

09:05 Right now, let me turn my right blinker on and pull off to the side of the road and introduce another of the more colorful and memorable warlords. This was Féng Yùxiáng, the Christian Warlord, as I mentioned at the end of the last episode. He was converted in 1913 or 1914 and became a devout Methodist.

09:26 It's said he saw this conversion to Christianity as a bridge to cooperation with the Westerners. But whether or not that's true is questionable. He was a very devout Christian till his dying day in 1948.

09:41 Féng Yùxiáng is the one who is remembered in popular Chinese history as the general who used to perform mass baptism ceremonies with his troops using a fire hose, although no one ever caught that on video and it's one of those George Washington chopping down the cherry tree kind of things. Mighta happened, probably didn't. I thought I saw a photo once.

10:04 Féng Yùxiáng, I'm sure you'll not be surprised to learn, was another product of Yuán Shìkǎi's Běiyáng organization, joining in 1902. He came from a military background. His father was an officer in the Qīng Imperial Army. Both parents, it's said, were opium addicts. As the tale goes Féng Yùxiáng, aged eleven, joined Lǐ Hóngzhāng's Huái Army. Nothing much to say except Féng Yùxiáng had the right stuff and was popular with his fellow soldiers. When his chance came, he joined the Běiyáng Army.

10:41 If you've ever seen photos of Féng Yùxiáng you'll agree, he was a pretty big guy, quite massive physically. And he knew how to keep a crowd riveted with his speaking style and the things he spoke about. He was an emotional man and would even weep during public speeches and addressing his troops. Unlike all his other warlord friends and foes, Féng Yùxiáng didn't hold one single base as a personal stronghold. So he tended to move around a lot, wherever the opportunities were.

11:14 And he was a no-frills simple soldier and made a big deal about his simplicity and the acetic lifestyle he professed. He traveled in freight cars or trucks and seemed to have never accumulated a warlord's wealth. He wasn't an educated man in the Confucian sense, but he was self-educated which is sometimes just as good.

11:38 Féng Yùxiáng was very strict and demanded a lot from his troops. He had this thing about reconciling Christian morals and Chinese militarism. He was a fitness fanatic in the Teddy Roosevelt style, and he insisted his officers and troops maintain a very tough exercise and training regimen.

12:01 You know, being a run of the mill foot soldier in a warlord army didn't necessarily make one the lowest of the low. But in 1920s Chinese society, it wasn't something that was looked up to either. But Féng Yùxiáng's troops, they were the exception. By reputation they didn't smoke or drink. He had a very strict prohibition against gambling and prostitution. He didn't even like foul language to be used. And if you wanted to rise up the ranks in Féng Yùxiáng's army, you had to do it by proving yourself to everyone.

12:35 He taught Christian and Confucian values to his troops and genuinely tried to help them. Along the way he established charitable organizations, orphanages, rehab centers for opium addicts. By the way, most all of these warlords got into the opium business, seeing how profitable and lucrative it was. This plague on society made a nice big comeback during the warlord years.

13:04   And when Féng's men weren't engaged in battle, he occasionally had them doing civil engineering projects like road building and irrigation, flood control. But as I said, he wasn't a warlord who was associated with any one particular province or area in China. So a lot of good that he tried to do never made it to the finish line. Like most of these militarists, their expertise sort of ended with military matters and not with things that involved civil society, public institutions and organizations.

13:38   During the decade from 1911 to 1921, Féng Yùxiáng saw a ton of action. He was always fighting somewhere. His career rose and fell along the way depending on how the ball bounced. I guess you can say Féng Yùxiáng always kept his options open. And when he made a promise to a potential ally, he often had his fingers crossed behind his back. But for this second major conflict that was brewing between Zhílì and Fèngtiān, he had initially hitched his wagon to Wú Pèifú and the Zhílì Clique.

14:16   And I mentioned before that the Western nations, they leaned in the direction of Wú Pèifú. And Zhāng Zuòlín, he was the favorite of the Japanese. Well, Féng Yùxiáng had become the darling of the Soviets. And just like with Wú Pèifú, Féng Yùxiáng also made the cover of Time Magazine, four years after Wú, in July 1928. So you know he's gonna be around for a while.

14:42 Féng Yùxiáng and Wú Pèifú, though initially on the same side, still had their differences. But after Wú pulled rank on Féng and had him demoted following some incident, Féng Yùxiáng wasn't happy and made it a point to get even.

15:02 And Wú Pèifú had other headaches as well. His Zhílì ally and titular head of the organization Cáo Kūn, was carrying out measures that prevented Wú Pèifú from entering Beijing to start putting the house in order and getting the government setup how he wanted to. So these two were at loggerheads.

15:20 When the Second Zhílì Fèngtiān War broke out in mid September 1924, Féng Yùxiáng was still on the Zhílì side, or so Wú Pèifú thought. Not only did he have a bone to pick with Wú Pèifú, Féng Yùxiáng also wasn't so happy with Cao Kun and all the promises made to him of money and support that wasn't forthcoming.

15:42 There had been a number of wars by the time: Zhílì-Anhui, the First Zhílì-Fèngtiān War plus other significant battles in central China and in the south and southwest. But this Second Zhílì-Fèngtiān War, this was the biggest one to date. We may call those weapons they had kid stuff compared to what's around today. But these warlord armies were equipped with what was the state of the art in 1924-1925. It was terrible to behold in action.

16:14 Here's how it all played out.

16:16 Riding on the outrage of Cáo Kūn's purchase of the presidential office in 1923-1924 the Ān-Fú Club, Duàn Qíruì's political organization, they were down but not out and still had a degree of power and influence in Shāndōng and parts of the lower Yángzǐ region. They along with Sun Yat-sen's KMT had begun having friendly discussions with Zhāng Zuòlín up in Manchuria.

16:44 As soon as Wú Pèifú got wind of this, he started stressing out, and for good reason too. He had his chief enemy Zhāng Zuòlín close by in China's northeast. With the KMT and Anhui Clique joining together and casting their lot in with Zhāng Zuòlín, Wú Pèifú knew he'd be looking at a potential two front war now.

17:06 This is where Lú Yǒngxiáng and Qí Xièyuán enter the story. Two more names for you. They're important to the story but generally not remembered as headliners from this era. No need to do any deep or shallow dives except to say Lú Yǒngxiáng was military governor of Zhèjiāng and was an Ānhuī Clique man, still loyal to Duàn Qíruì. Wú Pèifú wanted to get rid of him. Qí Xièyuán was the military governor next door in Jiāngsū and also was a Zhílì guy. He was Wú Pèifú's horse in this race.

17:45 Whichever warlord controlled Shanghai, got a piece of that action, not to mention the arsenal of weapons stashed there to protect foreign and Chinese commercial interests.

17:56 Here was the rub. Shanghai, on paper back then, was considered to be under the jurisdiction of Jiāngsū province. The Jiāngsū governor, Qí Xièyuán, was supposed to be the top voice in Shanghai. But Lú Yǒngxiáng, next door governor in Zhèjiāng, he had set himself up as the decider in Shanghai.

**18:17** Wú Pèifú backed Qí Xièyuán in this fight with the Zhèjiāng governor and Anhui Clique supporter, Lú Yǒngxiáng. In this inevitable showdown, Qí Xièyuán was backed by Wú Pèifú and Lú Yǒngxiáng had Zhāng Zuòlín's Fèngtiān backing.

**18:36** Though rivals, these two warlords, Lú Yǒngxiáng and Qí Xièyuán, they went to some trouble to keep the peace between their two respective provinces. But on September 3, 1924 the cracked facade of their cooperation finally broke away. The prize at stake was the political and economic control over China's most important commercial city and biggest cash cow, not to mention the vast arsenal of weapons stored there. Qí Xièyuán being a Zhílì warlord, had the support of the Zhílì Clique and with this kind of firepower he was able to pose a challenge to Lú Yǒngxiáng.

**19:18** And Sūn Chuánfāng down in Fújiàn was called up to assist fellow Zhílì comrade Qí Xièyuán. With Sūn's army attacking from the south, and after a lot of blood was spilled on both sides the Zhílì-backed Qí Xièyuán was able to overcome the Zhèjiāng forces of the Ānhuī and Fèngtiān-backed Lú Yǒngxiáng. This was all happening in early September 1924. By mid-October 1924 Lú Yǒngxiáng waved the white flag. Like other militarists before him, he escaped to Japan to wait things out and get back into the game at the right time.

98

19:59    So the Zhílì man, Qí Xièyuán prevailed with a little help from his friends and the main mission was accomplished of muscling Lú Yǒngxiáng out of Zhèjiāng and Shanghai. For his troubles,The governorship of Zhèjiāng was handed to Sūn Chuánfāng where he held sway till the end of 1926.

20:21    Following this victory by Qí, a joint expedition with the Ānhuī, Fèngtiān and Féng Yùxiáng military assets, was sent down to Zhèjiāng to deal with that situation. Leading that fight for the team was Zhāng Zōngchāng, the Dogmeat General.

20:39    This victory in the Jiāngsū-Zhèjiāng War did a lot to raise Sūn Chuánfāng up as another major warlord on a national scale. Thanks to his victories and a little good fortune here and there, Sūn found himself the warlord of Fújiàn, Jiāngxī and with this defeat of Lú Yǒngxiáng's forces, Zhèjiāng as well. And if you look at a map of China, those three contiguous provinces covered a lot of territory.

21:09    And while all this was going on in Jiāngsū and Zhèjiāng provinces, Zhāng Zuòlín had been having top secret discussions with all his closest generals about how best to take down Wú Pèifú and the entire Zhílì Clique.

21:27    This Jiāngsū-Zhèjiāng War was a bloody one. Inside the International Settlement in Shanghai they had to go all out to try and keep the fighting at bay as well as the wounded soldiers who needed hospitals and medical care. Residents of Shanghai all knew this fighting was

99

going on and they tried not to get caught up in it. It was okay to read about the fighting and the violence, but Shanghai residents didn't want to see it up close or from a distance. So now there was a new power that the enemies of the Zhílì Clique had to contend with. This was Sūn Chuánfāng, the Nanking Warlord as he became known.

22:08 Sūn Chuánfāng, he was another Shāndōnger and like almost everyone else of his ilk, came up through the Běiyáng Army organization. He got his start fighting for Wáng Zhànyuán. You remember this Húběi warlord from Part 3. Wáng Zhànyuán was one of the Zhílì warlords which by extension made Sūn Chuánfāng a Zhílì man, too, from way back. Long story short, he had done well and Sūn's first big break came when he was appointed the military governor of Fújiàn.

22:41 Qí Xièyuán, the Jiāngsū warlord, he didn't get to enjoy his big win in Shanghai too long. As I said, Zhāng Zuòlín sent his secret weapon, the Dogmeat General, down to Zhèjiāng and he got rid of Qí, forcing him to also take a Tokyo vacation, leaving his military assets to Sūn Chuánfāng. Zhāng Zōngchāng, the Dogmeat General. We're going to save him for next episode. He had quite a life. And besides all the claims to fame that he is remembered for in popular Chinese history, he was also a very hard to defeat opponent on the battlefield. And he was on the Fèngtiān team. We'll look closer at him next episode.

**23:24** So Zhāng Zōngchāng briefly took and held Jiāngsū and Shanghai starting in January 1925. And like I said, Qí Xièyuán tried to put up a fight but the help he was counting on from Sūn Chuánfāng never came, so he didn't get to enjoy being the top guy in Shanghai for too terribly long. Zhāng Zōngchāng kept a weary eye on Sūn Chuánfāng through 1925 and Sun finally ejects Zhāng Zōngchāng in the Fall of 1925 and Sūn Chuánfāng will be the greatest power in that Jiāngsū-Zhèjiāng-Shanghai region until the Northern Expedition in 1927. For now the voice that mattered in Jiāngsū, Fujian, Anhui and Jiāngxī belonged to Sūn Chuánfāng. He setup his HDQ in Nanjing and that's why his nickname in the press was the Nanjing or Nanking Warlord.

**24:23** And as I said, at the start of this First Jiāngsū Zhèjiāng War, Zhāng Zuòlín was already starting to prime the pump for his conquest. It had been two years since the thrashing he got at the hands of Wú Pèifú. But he laid low all this time and, like you've seen before in a hundred movies and novels, he got up off his knees and rebuilt, and trained and had invested in logistics, new military technologies including military aircraft. Now it was time for Zhāng Zuòlín to take what should have been his in 1922.

**25:04** These past similar showdowns had always taken place on the farthest southern fringes of Beijing and Tianjin and all the way east to Shānhǎiguān where the Great Wall meets the Yellow Sea. Tiānxià Dìyīguān as it says on the sign. The First Barrier under Heaven. Whoever controlled Shānhǎiguān controlled the railway that connected Zhāng Zuòlín's power base in Shěnyáng with Beijing.

25:34    This time around, the Second Zhílì Fèngtiān conflict was a little more spread out. But still mostly limited to northern Héběi, as Zhílì province would one day be called.

25:46    If you want to do a deep dive into the order of battle from start to finish, you will be met with a tidal wave of names of commanders, deputy commanders and battles splashed all over northern Hebei. Almost half a million combined troops on both sides. All the weapons of war that had caused all that horrible destruction on the battlefields of Europe during WWI, now these warlords were turning these mechanical devices on each other.

26:18    I think what's most important to know about the Second Zhílì Fèngtiān War was that, as I said, Zhāng Zuòlín had gone full boat for two years to train for this day. Wú Pèifú's Zhílì military organization was the overconfident incumbent.

26:35    The two things that caused Wú Pèifú to lose this war were perhaps his underestimating Zhāng Zuòlín's firepower and military effectiveness and for sure the defection of Féng Yùxiáng from the Zhílì side to the Fèngtiān side after hostilities had broken out.

26:55    That's a whole docudrama in and of itself, how Zhāng Zuòlín leading up to this moment in 1924 used his lieutenants to approach Féng Yùxiáng and make some attractive offers. He knew Féng was having issues with his boss Wú Pèifú which made him ripe for acquisition. And when some extra convincing was needed, Anhui Clique intermediaries approached Féng and sweetened the deal further with a two million yen cherry on top of everything else that had been promised. And when Féng Yùxiáng shook hands on that deal that spelled the end of Wú Pèifú and the Zhílì Clique as a major player in China.

27:40   Mid-September 1924, Zhāng Zuòlín's armies came face to face with those of Wú Pèifú. The armies collided right where Liáoníng meets Héběi, Zhílì province, near Shānhǎiguān, Qínhuángdǎo and in Chéngdé.

27:58   And then came the big moment, after fierce fighting on both sides that produced no clear winner so far, Féng Yùxiáng on October 22, 1924 launched his Beijing Coup. His great betrayal to Wú Pèifú and the whole Zhílì Clique. Here's where he pulls the rug out from under Wú. Féng's former boss Cáo Kūn, who famously bribed his way to the presidency, he was put under house arrest where he remained for two years. Feng's men then went on and took over all the levers of power in Beijing, as it happens in any coup d'etat.

28:39   Wú Pèifú did not see this coming. To say that Féng Yùxiáng's defection messed up his plans was a bit of an understatement. Despite walking into this war not fully prepared, he had held his own since the outbreak of the war, but now he was getting attacked on all sides and had to drastically change his military strategy mid-battle.

THE
CHP
CHINA HISTORY PODCAST
THE TRANSCRIPTS

THE WARLORD ERA
PART 6

Right when Wú Pèifú was desperately trying to turn the tide of the war, that's when he learned Féng Yùxiáng had defected and was now fighting against him.

29:14 Although the Japanese military didn't directly participate in this war, they put up that generous cash bribe that pushed Féng Yùxiáng over to the Fèngtiān side. Zhāng Zuòlín was the horse Japan had placed their bets on in this race. Wú Pèifú and the whole Zhílì military organization, they were intensely anti-Japanese. So for Japan, this Second Zhílì-Fèngtiān War was a big chance to achieve a nice political victory in China.

29:44 With Wú Pèifú in crisis, that's when everyone lined up against him came in for the kill.

29:51 In the end, Wú Pèifú and his remaining few thousand troops had to carry out a full-scale retreat to central China where he could rest easy under the care of his Zhílì ally, Sūn Chuánfāng.

30:06 To the victors, Zhāng Zuòlín and Féng Yùxiáng, they were now the kings of the north. Féng Yùxiáng had formed his own clique. With this victory he had hit the big time on the China national stage. In addition to the Christian Warlord, he was now known as the "Betrayer General". But look at everything he had now! He called this new clique the Guómínjūn. That translates to the National People's Army.

30:35 And I know you're going to find this hard to believe, but before long, Zhāng Zuòlín and his partner in the Second

Zhílì Fèngtiān War Féng Yùxiáng, they too, in less than a year turn on each other. And that's all for Part 7 coming up in a mere two weeks.

**30:54** I can't say our story is almost over, but we'll get to that Northern Expedition maybe by Part 8 or 9. This is Laszlo Montgomery, once again, signing off from the city of Los Angeles here in the Golden State, hoping you'll all keep an open mind to coming back again next time for another exciting episode of the Chinese History Podcast.

# The Warlord Era
# Part 7

## SUMMARY

In this Part 7 episode, the decade of battling warlords is coming to an end. Anhui and Zhili, then Zhili and Fengtian, and then Zhili and Fengtian again. We'll Laos cover the last of these series of clashes between warlords contending for supremacy in China, the Anti-Fengtian War. After 1925, everyone had had enough with these military governors. Was anyone going to step up and take them on and deal with the warlords once and for all?

## TRANSCRIPT

| | |
|---|---|
| 00:00 | Good evening everyone, Laszlo Montgomery here. Thanks for tuning in to the China History Podcast. Part 7 this time in our award-winning series which does a nice shallow dive into the main history surrounding the Warlord Era in China. |
| 00:16 | Last time we made it as far as the end of the Second Zhílì-Fèngtiān War. It turned out a little bit better for Zhāng Zuòlín this time around. He and the Betrayer General, Féng Yùxiáng joined forces to send Wú Pèifú running to the Nanking Warlord, Sūn Chuánfāng, for protection and to regroup. And even though he got walloped in this war with Zhāng Zuòlín, Wú Pèifú hasn't been written out of the script yet. |

00:44 | In this second encounter with the Manchurian Warlord, Wú Pèifú's best laid plans did not work out as he had hoped. Remember last time there were two things that blended into each other. First there was the Jiāngsū-Zhèjiāng War and that moved up the timetable for Wú Pèifú and forced his hand to enter this war with Zhāng Zuòlín half-cocked.

01:09 | Wú Pèifú and his Zhílì military were counting on a certain concatenation of events to happen in such a way that when the last move was made, he'd be left on top. He had tried to buy off the Anhui Clique to get them on his side. Though no longer a military threat, Duàn Qíruì's organization still had a solid power base in Shanghai and the lower Yangzi region. That didn't work out either. So, Duàn ended up siding with Zhāng Zuòlín.

01:41 | Wú Pèifú also was counting on making overtures to bring Sun Yat-sen and his whole Canton government organization over to the Zhílì side. This would leave Zhāng Zuòlín isolated in the northeast, ready to be taken down at a time of Wú Pèifú's choosing.

02:01 | But it didn't end up that way either. The prospective allies Wú Pèifú was hoping to attract sided with his enemy. And in Sun Yat-sen's case, got tied down dealing with local emergencies. And the Second Zhílì Fèngtiān War ended up being a massive military defeat for Wú Pèifú and the entire Zhílì organization.

02:26 | After he had won and all the dust settled from this Second Zhílì-Fèngtiān War, Zhāng Zuòlín had to set up another provisional government. I don't know which one this was since 1912. This was one of the hallmarks of the Warlord Era in China, the revolving doors in the halls of power in the Beijing government. And through this control of the government in Beijing came control of tax revenues which allowed them to wear the ring of legitimacy in front of the Chinese people and the foreign powers.

02:59 | Winning the war was easy for Zhāng Zuòlín compared to figuring out a way to divide up the spoils with Féng Yùxiáng. That was going to be awkward. Zhāng Zuòlín was much stronger than Féng Yùxiáng so he ended up with the good areas and Féng Yùxiáng got stuck with Súiyuǎn, Cháhār and Gānsù. Súiyuǎn and Cháhār were old provinces located adjacent to each other in what is today parts of Inner Mongolia where all the action is: Bāotóu, Hohhot, Ordos, and Wūhǎi.

03:32 | And you thought he'd never bounce back from those Nishihara loans, but Duàn Qíruì was installed as Provisional Chief Executive of this new government. Zhāng Zuòlín, Féng Yùxiáng and Lú Yǒngxiáng had all met in Tiānjìn in November 1924 to talk this idea over with Duàn Qíruì. Though not ideal, Duàn was the least despised and best compromise candidate available at the time.

04:02 | And in a grand gesture that meant well but didn't turn out as anyone hoped, Sun Yat-sen was invited by this new government to come to Beijing and confer with Zhāng Zuòlín, Féng Yùxiáng and others about reconciliation and unification of the country. By the end of 1924 when this invitation came, Sun Yat-sen was already fifty-eight years old and not in good health. He didn't know it yet, but he had end stages cancer already. But he took these warlords up on their offer and made the trip anyway. And when he got to Běijīng, he saw a doctor and was diagnosed with cancer and given days to live. Despite that, he hung in there until March 12, 1925 and then Sun Yat-sen was gone.

04:55 That was a body blow to the KMT. Now who were the warlords supposed to negotiate with? I won't get into it here, but there were a few men who had been quietly clamoring for the mantle of Sun Yat-sen in these final months. One of course, was Chiang Kai-shek. The others were Wāng Jīngwèi and Hú Hànmín. There's going to be an old-fashioned power struggle and you all know who prevails in the end.

05:20 Meanwhile up in the north of China, everyone knew it was bound to happen sooner or later. Relations between Zhāng Zuòlín and Féng Yùxiáng began to deteriorate. And as it happens these two rivals and their respective cliques, the Guómínjūn and the Fèngtiān, they were going to end up battling it out, just like Anhui and Zhílì, and Zhílì and Fèngtiān. Now came the next of these major wars of the era, the Anti-Fèngtiān War, also called the Third Zhílì-Fèngtiān War.

05:56 In the lead-up to this war both Féng Yùxiáng and Zhāng Zuòlín separately, sent envoys to Wú Pèifú, seeking his alliance in their war against the other. His army wasn't what it used to be but Wú Pèifú could still put together a sizable force.

06:13 | Who did Wú Pèifú side with? He had already faced down Zhāng Zuòlín twice. He beat him the first time and now, thanks to his defeat at the hands of the Manchurian Warlord, Wú Pèifú was in much reduced circumstances compared to the salad days of 1922-1924, and living off the kindness of Sun Chuanfang.

06:36 | But despite all that bad blood between Wú Pèifú and Zhāng Zuòlín, what Féng Yùxiáng had done to the Jade Marshal, Wú Pèifú... that really stuck in his craw. And Wú Pèifú wanted his revenge against this Betraying General. And he didn't want to wait until this dish was served cold. So Wú Pèifú joined hands with enemy Zhāng Zuòlín to put an end to Féng Yùxiáng.

07:04 | One thing the Zhílì and Fèngtiān Cliques had going for themselves was access to the sea. That meant importing foreign armaments was a heck of a lot more convenient for them. In Suíyǎn and Cháhā'ěr, Inner Mongolia? That's pretty far inland. Not too many seaports.

07:21 | But it was quite close to the Soviet Union. And the Soviets by 1925 were heavy in the arms business. They made a lot of nice stuff and Féng Yùxiáng was one of their best customers.

07:33 | In China, from the late Qing military modernization programs, to the whole long drawn out Warlord Era and all the way up through the end of the Civil War in 1949, the arms industry truly feasted in China.

07:50 Féng Yùxiáng set up his headquarters in Zhāngjiākǒu, to the northwest of Beijing. This city is also known in Chinese history by its Mongol name, Kalgan. His contact for Soviets arms and munitions was Michael Borodin of the Comintern. I should do an episode on him. In February 1925, Féng Yùxiáng had been receiving all these Russian weapons shipped via the Trans-Siberian and via old fashioned caravans pulling five hundred carts of rifles, carbines, machine guns, hand grenades and tens of millions of rounds of ammo. So when it was time to face off against Zhang Zuolin on the ancient northern plains of China, he was gonna be fully locked and loaded.

08:37 For this 3rd Zhílì Fèngtiān War or Anti-Fèngtiān War, it all kicked off in October 1925 when one of Zhāng Zuòlín's most trusted, but later thoroughly disgruntled generals, Guō Sōnglíng, turned on him and besieged the seat of power in the Fèngtiān Clique, the city of Shěnyáng. For this fight, General Guō thought he was getting some pre-arranged support from Féng Yùxiáng. But when it came to promises, these warlords often couldn't count on each other. And this is what happened here. After being left in the lurch in his three-month mutiny against Zhāng Zuòlín, for Guō Sōnglíng, it ended on the night before Christmas when the siege was lifted. This turncoat general Guō Sōnglíng and his wife too, they were captured and shot.

09:29 And with this act, it spelled the end to the ill-fated alliance between The Manchurian Warlord and the Christian Warlord. Féng Yùxiáng had not only betrayed his first ally Wú Pèifú, but his second one as well, Zhāng Zuòlín.

09:45  Guō Sōnglíng's defeat in Shěnyáng was a huge setback for Féng Yùxiáng as taking this stronghold of Zhang Zuolin was pretty central to his overall plan. Then from that point on into 1926, it was all downhill for the Christian Warlord. Wú Pèifú had had his revenge. With the armies of Zhāng Zuòlín, Wú Pèifú, the Dogmeat General Zhāng Zōngchāng and other warlords I haven't mentioned, all bearing down on Féng Yùxiáng, he hopped on the next available transport to Russia, announced his retirement and remained there for a stretch until Chiang Kai-shek's people come knocking on his door.

10:29  So now with bitter enemies Zhāng Zuòlín and Wú Pèifú victorious together in battle against their common foe, Féng Yùxiáng, together they had to figure out a way to govern the north and do that unification thing too while they were at it. This of course, was doomed from the start.

10:48  And by now, 1925-1926, everyone from the top down in Chinese society from the villagers to the hipsters in all the foreign enclaves in all the major cities, everyone had grown so sick of these warlords. Almost a decade of trying to bump each other off for the sake of seizing control of Beijing had injured, killed and profoundly disrupted the lives of too many people. The organized popular resistance to warlord rule really started to become more widespread.

**11:27**　You remember from many past episodes the May 30th Movement, May 30, 1925, that began up in Shanghai. A lot of this popular discontent was expressed through all kinds of protests. And many were directed at these jūnfá. That word was sort of a pejorative for these kinds of militarists. This is where the word "warlord" started to be bandied about more contemptuously in the foreign press. The literature that was floating around intellectual circles pulled no punches in its condemnation of the warlords and the lasting damage they were doing to the country.

**12:05**　By now, the idea of forming a national army and taking it to these regional strongman, well it wasn't so hard sell to anyone, except the warlords. This notion of mobilizing an army, marching north and defeating these self-serving warlords who had so abused their positions, this is where the idea for the Northern Expedition came. We're almost there.

**12:31**　Let's talk about a warlord I've mentioned a couple times but haven't given you his one-of-a-kind story. This was Zhāng Zōngchāng. And in talking about this most colorful and controversial of warlords we can go back and review a few of the events we've looked at these past episodes. He doesn't start to make headlines until 1925 and he sticks around till about 1929 and by 1932 he's gone.

**12:58**　Well, here's one more warlord for you, and I know you're gonna like him. Zhāng Zōngchāng, the Dog Meat General. The Gǒuròu Jiāngjūn. He didn't get that name because he liked to eat dog meat. Eating dog meat was the northeast China slang term for gambling on cards. Pai Gow, I'm guessing.

**13:16** Of all these warlords I've introduced and all their excesses, this one more than any other was the superlative. Even the great John King Fairbank, one of the most sacred of cows among Western Sinologists, called Zhāng Zōngchāng someone who "gave warlords a bad name".

**13:36** In today's popular history he's known for his various nicknames and a collection of anecdotes about the many antics attributed to Zhāng Zōngchāng during his military career.

**13:48** He was another Shāndōng guy. Born in Láizhōu 莱州 on the north Shāndōng coast west of Yāntái. Like Zhāng Zuòlín, he only had a couple years of formal education and accounts vary about his literacy. He was quite a poet later on life, in the, how shall I say, in the Andrew Dice Clay reciting Mother Goose kind of way. And this being a family program and all, I dare not treat you to any of the Dog Meat General's poetry.

**14:21** He didn't have a fancy military career like most of these other fellas we discussed. No national military academy for Zhāng Zōngchāng. His mother, this was part of his story too. He honored her to the max till his dying day. And it's said he took his beloved mother with him wherever he went except onto the field of battle. Back home in Shāndōng she was said to be a witch or some kind of exorcist back in her village. His father in most of the sources I found all agreed he was a head shaver by trade and played the trumpet. In other words, he didn't come from money.

15:00 The Dogmeat General, he had as hard-scrabble a childhood as you could get in a poor part of Shandong. He was huge. Fully grown he was 1.98 meters tall. That's 6'6" to my fellow Amerikanski's. He was a big guy. And around the turn of the century in that final decade of the Qing Dynasty, Zhāng Zōngchāng, like so many others who were dealt a similar hand in life, he turned to banditry as way to make a living.

15:30 If you did well and got noticed there was always the chance of promotion within these kinds of organizations. Zhāng Zōngchāng ended up fighting in Jiāngsū for the local warlord for a stint. He also saw action in the Russo-Japanese War, fighting on the side of the Russians. Later on in the 1920's he had an interesting relationship with the Russians and even kept, as a regiment in his army, a White Russian guard numbering about four thousand. He was famous for dressing up some of these troops in these old-style, loud and bodacious old Russian military uniforms. And he had a fair number of Russian concubines later on as well.

16:10 After serving in Jiāngsū without much to show for himself, he wandered north up to Manchuria. Zhāng Zuòlín's territory. He made a living on the streets of Harbin getting involved in more banditry as well as petty crime and I'm betting crimes that weren't so petty.

**16:28** Later on, after the Wǔchāng Uprising, he looked for opportunities in the Fèngtiān Army. He joined up and later on got himself noticed by Zhāng Zuòlín and in time gained the Manchurian Warlord's trust.

**16:45** One of the vignettes from Zhāng Zōngchāng's greatest hits package that got remembered or made up and passed down was the story of Zhāng Zuòlín's birthday party. Naturally all the men invited to celebrate with the great man, they were all trying to outdo each other in the extravagance of the gifts presented. As for Zhāng Zōngchāng, he no-showed first of all, and as his gift, he sent two empty coolie baskets and a pole accompanied with a note that said he would shoulder any responsibility given to him. He wanted to have a couple victories chalked up first before he was willing to stand before the Manchurian Warlord.

**17:26** Before we jump to his involvement in the aftermath of the Zhèjiāng-Jiāngsū War and afterwards when he became the warlord of Shāndōng, let's look at a few other anecdotes about Zhāng Zōngchāng.

**17:38** A Peking University president once described Zhāng Zōngchāng, when he was serving as the Dūjūn or military governor of Shandong as someone who "had the physique of an elephant, the brain of a pig and the temperament of a tiger."

**17:52** Time Magazine once called him the "basest warlord." James E Sheridan called him "…perhaps the best exemplification of the brutality and exploitation of which warlords were capable." One of his other nicknames was the Shandong Monster.

18:09 One of his more well-known atrocities that his troops engaged in was the game of "opening melons." That was a euphemism for splitting skulls open with swords. He was also a proponent of the idea of hanging severed heads of editors and journalists who criticized him from telegraph poles as warnings to others not to protest and to engage in a little self-censorship in what they printed. Members of secret societies, they too had their heads hung from the telegraph poles.

18:41 Interestingly he was also one of the earliest modern Chinese military organizations that incorporated women into the army.

18:49 But it was his harem and the conspicuousness with which he incorporated these women into his whole persona that made him so hard to forget. His harem consisted of something like forty women. The number varies. Someone reported they were from twenty-six different nationalities. And each one had a number and the flag of the woman's nation imprinted on her wash basin. They accompanied Zhāng Zōngchāng to various public and private affairs and banquets and served as hostesses at his extravagant parties. He could not remember their names and referred to them by the numbers assigned to them.

19:27 And speaking of numbers, although I contemplated leaving this out, again, the CHP being this long-running family program that it is. Zhāng Zōngchāng also had a couple other nicknames. Old 86 and Old 63 because if you took a stack of 63 Yuán Shìkǎi dollar coins or 86 silver dollars and piled 'em up on on top of the other, the stack of coins would add up to the length of the Dogmeat General's you know what.

**19:56** Later on, he acquired the nickname 72 Cannon Zhang. This arose out of an incident in 1929-1930 when Shāndōng province was gripped by this famine caused by lots of sun and no rain. Something this big was a job for Zhāng Zōngchāng. It was said he first visited the temple where the god was housed who was responsible for the weather. Rather than lighting up some incense and saying a prayer or two he took his big meaty hands and slapped the statue of the god repeatedly, berating him for causing this natural calamity and causing such hardship to the people of his province, Shāndōng.

**20:38** It's said he ordered one of his artillery units to fire into the clouds. And they did this seventy-two times before all that silver iodide started reacting with the clouds and the rain started falling.

**20:51** He was also known as the "Three Don't Knows" General. The Sān Bù Zhī Jiāngjūn. The three things he didn't know if you asked him was how many women in his harem, how much money he had, and how many troops under his command. The Three Don't Know's, ladies and gentlemans.

21:10 | He chain smoked Manila cigars, the Cuban's of Asia. And I have it on good authority he was also a big fan of the opium pipe.

21:19 | The great writer and all-around man of letters Lín Yǔtáng wrote an essay called "In Memoriam of the Dogmeat General" that was written on the morning Zhāng Zōngchāng died September 3, 1932. Let me just lift a few quotes from this work. Lín Yǔtáng wrote of him, "[He was] the most honest and unashamed of all the colorful, legendary medieval, and unashamed rulers of Modern China. He was direct, forceful, terribly efficient at times, obstinate and gifted with moderate intelligence. He made no pretenses to being a gentleman. He was ruthlessly honest, and this honesty made him much loved by all his close associates. If he loved a woman, he would say so, and he would see foreign consuls with a Russian girl sitting on his knee. If he held orgies, he didn't try to conceal them from his friends and foes. If he coveted his subordinate's wife, he told him openly and wrote no psalm of repentance about it like King David. And he was always square. If he took his subordinate's wife, he made her husband chief of police in Jìnán. Because of his honesty and his generosity, he was beyond the hatred of his fellow men. The morning I entered my office and informed my colleagues of the great news, everyone smiled, which showed that everyone was friendly towards him. No one hated him and no one could hate him. China was by then still being ruled by men like him, who hadn't his honesty, generosity and loyalty. He was a born ruler such as modern China wants, and he was the best of them all."

**23:05** For all his eccentricities, brutality and depravity, he was one of Zhang Zuolin's better generals. He was a fighter. More of his antics later.

**23:15** Last episode in Part 6, we discussed the Zhèjiāng-Jiāngsū War and how that tied in to the Second Zhílì Fèngtiān War. Zhāng Zōngchāng had fought for Zhāng Zuòlín and Team Fèngtiān, which included Duàn Qíruì and his Ānhuī Clique. For a job well done, scoring a number of victories in this most destructive war to date in this warlord era, Duàn and Zhang Zuolin saw to it that Zhāng Zōngchāng was made the military governor of Shāndōng and it was during this time, as warlord of Shandong, that most of the legend of the Dogmeat General got written.

**23:57** Prior to his stint as Dūjūn of Shandong, he briefly held things together in Shanghai for Zhāng Zuòlín. For the brief period he was there, party-goers and lovers of vice had a mini golden age. It was said Zhāng Zōngchāng and Zhāng Zuòlín's son, the Young Marshal, Zhāng Xuéliáng, those two partied together like it was 1999. They got high smoking opium, and visited all the night spots that were all part of the mystique of 1920s Shanghai. He was chums with Big Eared Dù. We remember him, Dù Yuèshēng, boss of the Green Gang, the most powerful crime syndicate in Shanghai.

**24:39** All those gangsta's got on famously with Zhāng Zōngchāng, as you could imagine. The vice trade in 1920s Shanghai was already not doing too bad. For the short period between the end of the Second Zhili-

Fèngtiān War, until Zhāng Zōngchāng left for Shandong in April 1925, those who enjoyed the seamy underside of Shanghai society, so wonderfully and colorfully depicted in Paul French's book from 2018 "City of Devils," they got to really let it all hang out without limits.

**25:15** Well, that's the Dogmeat General, 72 Cannon Zhang, Old 86 and a host of other epithets for this eccentric and sometimes quite amusing, but otherwise brutal, violent, impulsive man who, despite all that, had the loyalty and respect of his troops. And who, more often than not, delivered for his boss Zhāng Zuòlín.

**25:42** And the Old Marshal, he took care of Zhāng Zōngchāng and as I said, gave him the magnificent and historic province of Shandong to govern as warlords do. And most of the worst stories about his brutality and some of the more unsavory things attributed to him happened during this period that ended in May 1928.

**26:04** After the Anti-Fèngtiān War ended and Fèngtiān emerged as the winner, that's pretty much it as far as this ten-year spate of intra-warlord warfare involving all these militarists and their minions fighting each other.

**26:21** And everything is going to reach a crescendo in the Northern Expedition which will be led by Generalissimo Chiang Kai-shek. And for the balance of this series we'll focus on that final chapter of the Chinese Warlord Era. The final chapter but not the epilog. There will still be the Central Plains War but trust me, there's still more to come.

26:42 | Okay, Laszlo Montgomery here signing off from Los Angeles on a nice rainy day. The snow on the San Bernardino Mountains looks great, like a postcard. You should come out and see it. Please think about joining me again next time for another exciting episode of the China History Podcast.

# The Warlord Era
# Part 8

**THE TRANSCRIPTS**

## SUMMARY

Part 8 in this series first presents a brief overview of "The Model Governor" Yan Xishan and his home province of Shanxi. After some daring moves on Chiang Kai-shek's part, he bests his opponents and takes control of the KMT and the National Revolutionary Army. Under his command, Chiang launches the Northern Expedition. This episode will focus on the fateful years of 1926-1927.

## TRANSCRIPT

| | |
|---|---|
| 00:00 | Welcome back again everyone, Laszlo Montgomery here. The China History Podcast, Part 8 today, The Chinese Warlord Era. You can be sure everyone in China has had enough of these warlords, and starting in this episode it's time to take them down. |
| 00:18 | But before we go there, allow me to pull over once again and introduce you to one more major heavy of the warlord era. This was Yán Xīshān. When you think of the most well-known names from this era, Yán Xīshān always makes the list. He was a marquee name from the Warlord Hall of Fame. |
| 00:38 | Well, if that's true, why is it we're already eight episodes into this series and we've hardly heard his name? And it's already 1925-1926. Where's he been hiding |

THE
CHP
CHINA HISTORY PODCAST
THE TRANSCRIPTS

THE WARLORD ERA
PART 8

out? Well, Yán Xīshān wasn't hiding out and like his warlord brethren he'd already been the master of his own province since 1917. He was the warlord of Shānxī. And in saying that, if you're familiar with that laid-back northern province, famous for it noodles and natural resources, you'll know why.

01:11 If you look at a physical map of China, although Shānxī's main city of Tàiyuán is only two hundred miles away from Beijing, it may as well be two thousand. Today, of course you can take the high speed train that runs between Tàiyuán and Běijīng. Two and a half to three hours is all it'll take you. But back in the 1920's and 30's, in Yán Xīshān's day, that was a much greater distance.

01:37 Shānxī province is surrounded on all sides by mountains and rivers. The Wŭtái, Tàiháng and Zhōngtiáo Mountains. And of course the Yellow River flows along the southern and western borders of the province. Historically, all these natural barriers combined kept the province somewhat isolated from what was happening in the central plain of eastern China in Manchuria, Héběi, Hénán, Shāndōng and elsewhere.

02:09 Tradition said it was in Shānxī where Yŭ the Great of the Xià Dynasty tamed the flooding rivers. And the mythical emperor Yáo, who Confucius admired so greatly, also from Shānxī, the land where the ancient state of Jìn was located.

02:26 So its relative isolation contributed significantly to keeping Shānxī from being more directly engaged in all the history and goings-on elsewhere in post-imperial China. On the one hand Shānxī's geographic fate impeded the province's economic progress and easy access to the foreign traders who congregated in the major coastal cities and treaty ports. But on the other hand, for Yán Xīshān at least, this allowed him to keep all these rivalries and wars fought between Ānhuī, Zhílì, Fèngtiān, the KMT and the Guómínjūn far from his doorstep. All that action tended to be focused south and east of Yán Xīshān's realm.

03:15 Yán Xīshān never stayed loyal to one ally with any consistency. He changed partners wherever and whenever it benefited him. He was good at picking the right side and although not as powerful a player as some of his fellow warlords, his support was always sought out just like a minority party in government.

03:36 So that's why we haven't heard Yán Xīshān's name too much in this series. But let me tell you, he had quite an enterprise going up there in Shānxī, far from the madding crowd. He didn't turn Shānxī into a rich province but thanks to his efforts over the thirty-eight years he ran the place, he was certainly responsible for making it less poor.

03:58 But he knew, despite everything that he could do, his province wasn't in the same league militarily or economically as those to the east of him. The terrain of Shānxī also wasn't terribly suited for agriculture. But Shānxī province, it was good enough for Yán Xīshān. That's all he wanted. He was by no means a Zhāng Zuòlín or Wú Pèifú who both sought out national hegemony.

04:25    What's his story? Yán Xīshān was born in Xīnzhōu, just north of Shānxī's main city of Tàiyuán, the commercial, industrial and political center of Shānxī province. Not everyone knows this, but Shānxī was once one of the largest banking centers in China. And Yán Xīshān's family came from one of these well-off banking families. However, his family fell on hard times during the late Qīng and, Yán Xīshān did what a lot of young men did. Despite his family background and high degree of education, he enrolled in one of the many military academies popping up everywhere, this one in Tàiyuán.

05:07    From there, Yán Xīshān did the fashionable thing to do for many a budding militarist. He went to Japan and continued his studies at Japanese military academies. This five-year stint beginning in 1904 had a rather profound impact on Yán Xīshān and how he later on ran his province. Like countless other educated Chinese who had their eyes opened by the achievements of Japan and the other foreign powers, he vowed to implement many of these reforms in his home country. Even with his own troops later on he saw much in Japan's samurai legacy that he attempted to introduce.

05:51    Yán Xīshān's philosophy that he tried to instill in his troops and inside Shānxī melded militarism, nationalism, anarchism, democracy, capitalism, communism, individualism, imperialism, universalism and paternalism. How's that for a combination?

**06:14** | Whilst studying in Japan he met Sun Yat-sen and joined Sun's party, the Tóngménghuì or United League. He also was a close friend of fellow Shānxī native H.H. Kung, Kǒng Xiángxī, a KMT stalwart, finance minister, and spouse to one of the Soong Sisters, the oldest and brightest, Àilíng. H.H. Kung served as an early adviser to Yán Xīshān when he was just getting established up in Shānxī.

**06:47** | Although a Sun Yat-sen ally, Yán Xīshān didn't always see eye to eye with the KMT or the southern Canton government. Sun Yat-sen's failed Second Revolution that we discussed in a previous episode... Yán Xīshān didn't provide any support and, as he often did, he sat this conflict out. And to be truthful, like most of these warlords, Yán Xīshān wasn't too enthusiastic about Sun Yat-sen's political ideals. And the May Fourth Movement, he wasn't on the side of the students and demonstrators. Let's just say that this was a typical point of view shared by most all warlords.

**07:26** | After returning from Japan in 1909, Yán Xīshān joined the New Army and got assigned to his home province. At first Yán's loyalty was to Yuán Shìkǎi and the Běiyáng organization but later in 1913, he ran afoul of Yuán and had to keep a safe distance and bide his time until after Yuán died in 1916. Yán Xīshān had already taken over the role of military governor in Shānxī and like everyone else I mentioned, he was one of those who, after Yuán's death, transitioned from military governor to warlord.

**08:05** His record shows a lot of hits and misses. Shānxī today is China's West Virginia. The land of coal. That began with Yán Xīshān and his development of the province's coal and iron ore mines. He also promoted Shānxī's cotton industry and turned the province into a powerhouse in that industry.

**08:5** Like Féng Yùxiáng, Yán Xīshān tried to stamp out many old traditional practices. Cutting queues off men still sporting the Manchu hairstyle was one of them. He also implemented a whole slew of social reforms in Shānxī that clamped down mercilessly on purveyors of opium and other drugs as well as the practice of foot binding. He also promoted basic education for women. In 1918 he launched a program in Shānxī to educate young children. By 1923 as many as 800,000 Shānxī kids had been beneficiaries of this program. A big chunk of Shānxī's provincial budget went to education. Not to higher education, but to basic elementary schooling, reading and writing. Hey man, you had to walk before you ran.

**09:20** He was also a big proponent of water conservation and tree-planting as well as the propagation of TCM, Traditional Chinese Medicine. Two noted organizations he called for were the Early Morning Rising Society and the Heart Cleansing Institute. The names alone can give you an idea where his head was at. Clean disciplined living. He tried to propagate his philosophy through these institutes and build up the people's morality and positive living. He was no Dogmeat General.

09:52   In short, Yán Xīshān knew he was the ruler and master of one of China's less prosperous provinces and he was determined to lift his people up by embracing all that was good and useful from Japan and the West. This was particularly true with respect to science and medicine.

10:14   Thanks to Shānxī's remote location, he had been able to survive Yuán Shìkǎi, the whole Warlord Era, the Nationalist Era and later on, Japanese invasion and civil war with the Communists. He was a survivor. He was a close friend of Duàn Qíruì but never joined the Ānhuī Clique. He always kept Shānxī neutral. He was his own clique. And as I mentioned, even though he was friendly with Sun Yat-sen, he didn't want Sun's political ideas being implemented in his province.

10:46   And for all these reasons, Yán Xīshān acquired the nickname of "The Model Governor," the Mófàn Dūjūn. A lot of things went right under his leadership. But he had his share of headaches and financial crises brought on by speculation and ideas that were great and well-meaning but not implemented well.

11:08   In all the info written about Yán Xīshān he was described as solemn to the point of dour, unsmiling, very reserved in public gatherings, never laughed or revealed his inner feelings. You'd think he'd be a Feng Yuxiang type who espoused a plain and acetic lifestyle. But Yán Xīshān acquired massive amounts of wealth and lived a very luxurious lifestyle up in his home base of Tàiyuán. Robin Leach would have loved him.

11:41 So Yán Xīshān didn't just come out of nowhere. For the preceding seven episodes he's been playing in the background, quietly running his province and staying out of the major conflicts. As soon as we get to the Northern Expedition, however, as 1927 rolls around, Yán Xīshān came out from the shadows and began to play a more noticeable role in this Warlord Era. And as we get closer to that time, we'll revisit Yán Xīshān.

12:10 Let's take a quick look at what was cooking in the south. I want to stress again, from the moment the Qing Dynasty fell in 1911 up to these years we're in right now, 1925-1926, there was a whole other thang going on in the south of China with respect to the rival government based in Canton, or Guǎngzhōu. All those southern provinces had their own warlord happenings, over in Yúnnán, Guǎngdōng, Guìzhōu and Guǎngxī.

12:38 All this time since the Wǔchāng Uprising, 10-10-1911 the southern leadership hadn't been able to assemble any kind of coalition that could pose a serious challenge to these Běiyáng generals. Too much time had been wasted since 1917 trying to unify the leadership and to resist the actions of the northern warlords. And then once Sun Yat-sen died in 1925, it thrust the southern government into yet another political crisis.

13:10 Let's jump to March 20, 1926. This is the date of the Canton Coup. Chiang Kai-shek, down in Guǎngzhōu, still head of the Whampoa Military Academy. He received a tip that his life was in danger and his political enemies were going to forcibly remove him from the whole KMT organization. So Chiang didn't follow this up too much and took preemptive action against those he thought were plotting against him, the KMT Left and the Communists, aided and abetted of course by the Comintern.

13:45 This sham cooperation with the Chinese Communists and this whole United Front idea… I mentioned this in Part 6. Despite all the sweet talking from the Comintern, Chiang smelled a rat. All along and after this right-wing Canton Coup was carried out, he put an end to that arrangement and seized control of the government and the Nationalist Army.

14:09 His rival Wāng Jīngwèi, leader of the leftist faction of the KMT, after seeing that Chiang Kai-shek had gone and done, picked up and went on an extended European holiday. This move by Chiang was a serious blow to the KMT Left.

14:25 When the dust settled, the left wing of the Nationalist Party had been marginalized and Chiang got to halt this slow and steady infiltration of Russians and Chinese Communists into his organization. He didn't do anything violent so much as he just sidelined the communists. Chiang felt there was still a need for Soviet support with his Northern Expedition. So he didn't burn those bridges just yet.

14:51 And as for that short-lived experiment of civilian control over the military, Chiang put an end to that too.

14:58    Once this was achieved and Chiang had officially put on that mantle of Sun Yat-sen, it was going to be left up to him and his armies to get rid of all these Zhāng Zuòlín's, Wú Pèifú's, Yán Xīshān's, Féng Yùxiáng's, Zhāng Zōngchāng's, and all these other, well, whatever you wanna call them.

15:18    Almost from the very beginning, going back to the death of Yuán Shìkǎi in 1916, the solidarity of this Běiyáng Clique that Yuán had led, started to fall apart. Between 1917 and 1926, a total of nine years, these warlords tried wiping each other out. Then they'd join together to whack a common foe. And as soon as that was done they'd go back to trying to kill each other again. On and on it went. Year after destructive year, all over China. Not just in the north and central part of the country. Down in the south too.

15:54    And a few of these major figures, these leaders of these various cliques, not all, they had this idea in the back of their head to try and become that Qín Shǐhuáng or Líu Bāng who could best their rivals and become the last man standing to unify China into one nation, with them in charge.

16:16    I spared you all the political lead-up to the Canton Coup of March 1926. What's important to know for our story is that this is where Chiang Kai-shek takes the lead and becomes the one within the KMT to finally take this old idea first discussed by Sun Yat-sen and others in the early 1920s, to take the fight to these warlords and see it though to the end. These warlords had to be toppled or won over to the side of the KMT, the Guómíndǎng, the Nationalist Party. So you'll start hearing more and more of Chiang from here on out.

**16:52** And the men mostly getting in Chiang's way of Chinese unification were Zhāng Zuòlín, Wú Pèifú, Yán Xīshān. Zhāng Zōngchāng and Sūn Chuánfāng. These warlords in particular and their allies, they held sway over the government in Beijing, in Zhílì, Shāndōng, all of Manchuria, Hénán, Húnán, Húběi, Fújiàn, Jiāngxī, Ānhuī, Zhèjiāng and Jiāngsū. Chiang Kai-shek had his work cut out for him.

**17:27** So let's go back to the Canton Coup in March 1926. To give you a time stamp to what was happening up north when Chiang grabbed power in this right-wing coup, the Anti Fèngtiān War was just ending. You recall Zhāng Zuòlín and Wú Pèifú teamed up to overwhelm Féng Yùxiáng and knock him off the board for a little while. So while Chiang was making his move to take control of the KMT, Féng Yùxiáng was soon about to take a brief Russian holiday. And Zhāng Zuòlín was making himself comfortable in Beijing.

**18:01** On June 5, 1926 Chiang was named Commander-in-chief, the Zǒng sīlìng, of the National Revolutionary Army, the NRA. And then on July 1, 1926 the realigned Canton government issued this bold proclamation that stated, "To protect the welfare of the people, we must overthrow all warlords and wipe out reactionary power so that we may implement the Three People's Principles and complete the National Revolution."

**THE**
**CHP**
**CHINA HISTORY PODCAST**
**THE TRANSCRIPTS**

THE WARLORD ERA
PART 8

**18:34** From this point forward, just as Sun Yat-sen had once been called, now Chiang Kai-shek became the generalissimo.

**18:45** And with these favorable winds blowing in his sails, Chiang believed if there ever was a time to launch the Northern Expedition against the warlords, this was it. He didn't want to lose the momentum. The Northern Expedition in its scale, in the number of casualties and in its sheer destruction to infrastructure and private property was perhaps the biggest military campaign carried out anywhere between the two World Wars.

**19:15** The NRA was heavily outnumbered by troops fighting under the warlords when Chiang Kai-shek set out to fulfill his destiny on July 9, 1926.

**19:26** The plan was to take Húnán first and use that as a springboard into Húběi. And of course, the grand prize in Húběi were the tri-cities that made up Wǔhàn. That meant first going head to head with the powerful Húnán warlord, Táng Shēngzhì. Táng Shēngzhì was a Hunan born and raised graduate from the Bǎodìng Military Academy and had had a very active career in the military. But it was in Húnán province where he had made his mark. And Táng Shēngzhì was Chiang's first match.

**20:01** Except that Táng Shēngzhì welcomed Chiang and said from now on he was on the KMT side. Yeah, he wasn't the only one, too. Others will, for their own self-serving reasons as always, join the Northern Expedition on the NRA side and pledged their army and their "loyalty" to Chiang Kai-shek. And quotation marks around that word loyalty.

20:25 Besides Táng Shēngzhì there were also more than two dozen other mini-warlords scattered all around Húnán. That province was infested. The lower down the food chain you went, the less effective and more unruly these troops were. Those that didn't turn and run when they faced the NRA ended up as new recruits in Chiang's army. By June 11ᵗʰ, the capital Chángshā was taken, followed by the rest of Húnán by the end of July.

20:55 It had fallen on Wú Pèifú's shoulders to try and hang on to Húnán, but with Táng Shēngzhì defecting and troops from Guìzhōu and other smaller warlords given promises by Chiang for joining the KMT side, it was too overwhelming of a force. And they made fast work of Wú Pèifú in Húnán. They'll chase him all the way to Wǔhàn before he exits the fight and flees to his stronghold in Hénán.

21:23 And Yán Xīshān, the Shānxī Warlord, the Model Governor? He too signed up with Chiang Kai-shek in this Northern Expedition. He always knew his limitations and had survived for this long by picking the right friends at the right time. He had some amazing staying power. You know, several years later he, too, made the cover of Time Magazine's May 19, 1930 issue with the caption underneath: "China's Next President". That Henry Luce. He sure loved them warlords.

21:55 | Húběi province was next to fall at the end of October 1926. Thanks to two of his most trusted generals Hé Yìngqīn and Zhāng Qún, Fújiàn and Zhèjiāng too both fell into line. You can say the Northern Expedition was off to a blazing start. Chiang Kai-shek must have been feeling pretty good at this point. No one would dare challenge him politically now.

22:21 | But much of this great success in the first months of the Northern Expedition had come mostly by way of occupying territory that warlords had either vacated or turned over to Chiang. And although a lot of blood had been spilled, most of these spectacular gains weren't coming so much from winning on the battlefield. With all deals and mergers and acquisitions Chiang was making with these warlords to build a coalition, the KMT was sorta becoming the party of warlords.

22:52 | Chiang's attention next turned to Nánjīng and Shànghǎi. This is when he decided to move the military headquarters from Wǔhàn to closer to where the action was, in Nánchāng, Jiāngxī province. The KMT Left, they didn't like that because they wanted the center of power to remain in their stronghold of Wǔhàn. They didn't want to sit back and watch Chiang Kai-shek keep grabbing more power and control. So they openly challenged Chiang for his actions and stripped him of all powers.

23:24 | Up to now, militarily at least, everything had gone just fine and suddenly this political rift erupted. Chiang Kai-shek, as if he didn't know it already, had his suspicions confirmed that the KMT Left was not on his side and were in fact, against him, in cahoots with the Communists. And the Left saw what Chiang Kai-shek was doing, trying to consolidate all this power in his hands of the state, of the Party. And to them he was shaping up to be just another Yuán Shìkǎi.

**23:59**     I'm not sure if it was around now or maybe even earlier but Chiang Kai-shek had decided that not unless the KMT Left split from the Communists would he ever accept them. Chiang had let it be known that if Wāng Jīngwèi and his followers in Wǔhàn on the Left didn't purge their ranks of Communists and get on the Chiang Kai-shek bus, they'd be run over by it.

**24:25**     Then came the famous rambling Stalin telegram that gave all kinds of strange and terribly unrealistic instructions to the Communists in China about where to go from here. When Wāng Jīngwèi was shown a copy of these instructions from Stalin he realized that the KMT Left was only being used and that the Soviets had much darker and sinister plans as far as this pet Chinese communist project they had going on. In retrospect, we can say how could anyone not have known. But in 1926, nobody knew what we know now.

**25:00**     After a very bloody and costly series of battles with the forces of warlord Sūn Chuánfāng, on March 22, 1927 NRA forces led by Bái Chóngxǐ entered Shanghai. And at this very moment where Communist organizing was showing smashing signs of success all over not only Shanghai but in Wǔhàn, Guǎngzhōu and other cities as

THE
CHP
CHINA HISTORY PODCAST
THE TRANSCRIPTS

THE WARLORD ERA
PART 8

well, it was decided that the Communists and all their sympathizers needed to be rubbed out. And for all you that remember CHP episode number 55, what followed Bái Chóngxǐ's taking of Shanghai became known as the Shanghai Massacre.

25:42    Prior to the taking of Shanghai, at the end of February 1927, the Dogmeat General, Zhāng Zōngchāng had taken his private railway car, harem in tow, and rode in the direction of Shanghai. He brought his expensive coffin with him just in case. He blew into Shanghai prior to the arrival of Bái Chóngxǐ's troops. Old 86 was extravagantly feted at a party by Dù Yuèshēng himself. I wish I could have been a fly on the wall during that evening. Big Ears Du and the Dogmeat General? What a night that must have been.

26:20    But for all his toughness and his reputation, when he faced off against the NRA troops led by the often victorious Guangxi clique Muslim general Bái Chóngxǐ, it wasn't much of a fight. And the Dogmeat General's troops had grown flabbier and more undisciplined than ever. They fled and did what warlord soldiers always do in these situations. They tried to blend in the crowd and live to fight another day.

26:49    After the city had been taken, Chiang arrived in Shanghai on March 26, 1927. His first stop was to Big Ears Dù Yuèshēng's boss, Pockmarked Huáng, Huáng Jīnróng. I didn't mention this but all this time in late 1926 and into 1927, there had been massive civic unrest in the most important cities. From Guǎngzhōu to

Wǔhàn to Shanghai and elsewhere, organized labor was causing all kinds of economic chaos through strikes and boycotts. The communists, with their anti-imperialist, anti-West, anti-Japan and anti-warlord rhetoric had become emboldened with their success in organizing. And it was Chiang Kai-shek's intention to take them down a few notches. And to do this, Huáng Jīnróng was just the guy he needed.

27:48 Early morning on April 12,1927 came the fateful bugle call that signaled the commencement of the Shanghai Massacre, also known as Day One of the Chinese Civil War. There was no turning back after this event, that is, unless one side was threatened or cajoled by outside forces to call a truce.

28:10 With that nasty bit of business out of the way and the Communists driven deep underground, Chiang Kai-shek established a rival government of the Republic of China based in Nánjīng and this government was first chaired by Hú Hànmín. All Wāng Jīngwèi and his allies in Wǔhàn could do was to make a toothless attempt to expel Chiang from the KMT and charge him with a list of accusations like splitting the Party in the wake of the Shanghai Massacre. The Western nations were secretly relieved with this outcome. Order had at last been restored at last to commerce. All that was left over were the hard feelings.

28:50 As far as the northern warlords, they were notorious Chinese Communist haters too so they had no issues with what Chiang Kai-shek had carried out with the massacre and the White Terror that continued on unabated till it wasn't safe for any communist to come out of hiding.

29:07 To defend against what they knew was coming, the northern warlords led by Zhāng Zuòlín formed a coalition called the Ānguójūn, The National Peace Army.

29:18 Warlords from Zhèjiāng, Fújiàn, Shànghǎi, Nánjīng, parts of Ānhuī, Jiāngsū, most of Guǎngxī, Guǎngdōng and Sìchuān had gone over to the Chiang Kai-shek side. That sounds like a lot but it was hardly all of China. In fact, pretty much that was most everything south of the Yángzǐ River. Once again this mother of all rivers in China was going to have to be crossed for yet another military campaign.

29:49 And if not for their mutual hatred of leftists and communists, these former warlords and their tenuous new allies, the KMT, had very little in common politically or ideologically.

30:02 And up in Beijing around this very same time in late April 1927, not long after the Shanghai Massacre, Zhāng Zuòlín's men raided the Russian Embassy there and walked out with a trove of documents that exposed the Soviets' intentions as far as the Chinese Communists went. Nineteen Chinese communists including one of the ideological founders of the Party, Lǐ Dàzhāo, were captured inside the embassy and later executed. Lǐ Dàzhāo was one of Chairman Máo's early mentors at Peking University. An early casualty of the revolution, dead at the age of thirty-seven. Almost thirty-eight thousand dedicated communists and their supporters ended up losing their lives in the 1927 White Terror. It was a bad year for the CCP by any reckoning.

**30:56** Okay, let's hang it up for now and return to our story in a mere couple weeks. We'll pick up in these post Shanghai Massacre weeks and months and see what happens with the Northern Expedition and beyond.

**31:10** Okay, as far as our little warlord series, it's getting near the end. Let's try and finish this in ten episodes. Laszlo Montgomery here signing off as I have all year-long, from Los Angeles, California. Boy, not like the early days when I was on the run constantly. Please please me, like I please you, and come back one more time for another exciting episode of the China History Podcast. Take care, everyone!

# THE CHP
**CHINA HISTORY PODCAST**
**THE TRANSCRIPTS**

## The Warlord Era
## Part 9

## SUMMARY

As the Northern Expedition ramps up and the Warlord Era starts to wind down, there's still plenty of action and violence to go around. In this episode, we look at the events following the Shanghai Massacre when Chiang and his "ally" Wang Jingwei take the fight to Zhang Zuolin's northern warlord alliance. The Manchurian Warlord meets his explosive end in this episode.

## TRANSCRIPT

00:00 | Welcome back everyone, Thanks for tuning in to the China History Podcast. Laszlo Montgomery here for the 239th time.

00:11 | For the past eight episodes and for the 9th one today, we've been looking at the Warlord Era in China that began in Part 1 with the death of Yuán Shìkǎi in June of 1916. And in this episode, the penultimate one I guess you could call it, we'll almost but not quite finish things off as we continue on with the Northern Expedition, the big military campaign that was going to once and for all put an end to the warlords and let China, for the first time since the fall of the Qing, to get a chance to take a breather and regroup after a very rough half century. Wishful thinking back then.

00:52 We left off last episode in the afterglow of the Shanghai Massacre. This was in April of 1927. If you recall from so many past episodes and series, this was also when the Chinese Communist Party, the ones who survived that is, scattered in all directions and Máo Zédōng and his followers had all made their way to Jǐnggāngshān in Jiāngxī and started to create a bit of CCP history there.

01:20 And for the half year leading up to the Shanghai Massacre the labor and peasant movement had advanced greatly thanks to a number of factors. CCP organizing, help from the Comintern, reforms that followed in the wake of the first phase of the Northern Expedition and from the KMT Left as well. So, that problem was dealt with for the time being.

01:43 From about the Ānhuī-Zhílì War in July 1920 to the two Zhílì-Fèngtiān Wars of 1922 and 1924 followed by the Anti-Fèngtiān War of 1925-1926, and all of these other wars and mini wars, Jiāngsū-Zhèjiāng, Guǎngdōng-Guǎngxī, Yúnnán-Guǎngxī. Remember when I said at the outset what a terribly complicated period this was, from the moment Yuán Shìkǎi died in June 1916, it was a time of non-stop war, battles and skirmishes, alliances, broken alliances? The world at war, government in disarray, the CCP on the rise, the Soviets trying to control the narrative... the suffering of the entire Chinese populace who had to go along on this ride, this Warlord Era. It really was a rough dozen or so years before it finally ended and was replaced by something even more horrific.

02:46 I've left out quite a bit of history from this whole Warlord Era. It's a lot of the same thing. I've mentioned most of the important events and some of the major names. But this dive could go much much deeper than I'm taking it. And being the betting man that I have always been, I'm thinking most of you will be mostly satisfied with the headlines. The main thing I guess I wanted to convey was the destructiveness of these years. Not only to the land, the infrastructure and the people's livelihood, but to China's standing in the world.

03:20 Because of these warlords and all the political paralysis caused, China sort of boxed itself into a corner and made it easy for other nations to take advantage of the situation and get rich off the fat of the land.

03:34 And as we head deeper into 1927, 1928 and even into 1929 and 1930 you'll see, these warlords become like zombies that refuse to die. During the Northern Expedition, with every victory of the NRA, you keep getting the feeling this nightmare is at last over at last. And then, it's not over. They're back!

03:57 You know, when Chiang went and ordered the Shanghai Massacre, it was shocking. It created, what turned out to be, a rift between the leftist and rightist elements of the KMT that could never be truly reconciled. And of course, as far as KMT-CCP relations, Chiang Kai-shek going and doing what he did pretty much threw down the gauntlet. The CCP understandably was in total disarray and trying to bounce back from the Shanghai Massacre and the so-called White Terror. They had been taken by surprise and needed time to regroup and get back into the game later. At this point they were following the advice of their Soviet comrades and not yet taking control of their own destiny. That will come soon. In the meantime, Stalin and Trotsky were having their epic struggle up in Russia. And both had opposite points of view as far as which road the CCP should take in China.

04:56 The KMT Left and KMT Right went at each other. Wāng Jīngwèi called for Chiang's ouster and stripped him of all offices and commands. Chiang countered by setting up a new government in Nanjing on April 18, 1927. Stalin's famous rambling telegram of early June 1927 did a lot to complicate matters. I mentioned it last episode. And once Wāng Jīngwèi got to read a copy of what Stalin was suggesting that the CCP do, he knew the KMT Left was just a pawn being used by the CCP and their Soviet masters against the KMT Right.

05:37 So Wang had managed to alienate himself from Chiang and the KMT Right in Nanjing. And now he knew the ones he trusted all this time were secretly plotting against his interests.
So, what to do now?

05:53 The two competing factions of the KMT decided, not as one fighting force, but separately instead, to resume the fight against Zhāng Zuòlín and his National Pacification Army allies. On the KMT Left they had the Hunan Warlord Táng Shēngzhì as their main military backer. They decided to take the fight to Zhang, meet up with Féng Yùxiáng along the way, bring him over to their side, finish off Zhāng Zuòlín and his minions and then, once this was all taken care of, they planned to go after Chiang Kai-shek and get rid of him. Well, that was the plan anyway.

**06:33** The Wǔhàn coalition, led by Táng Shēngzhì and his army had marched northeast along the Peking-Hànkǒu railway line towards the city of Zhèngzhōu. All throughout May 1927 whenever they encountered Zhāng Zuòlín's troops, they kept pushing him back. All was going well so far.

**06:54** The Wǔhàn troops and Féng Yùxiáng's troops, who had marched from Shǎnxī, all converged on the ancient city of Zhèngzhōu about the same time. Féng Yùxiáng setup his headquarters there. Chinese civilization had been alive and well in that city in Hénán province going all the way back to the Shāng kings of the 16th century BCE, more than thirty centuries before Féng Yùxiáng added to this city's considerable historical legacy.

**07:24** Zhèngzhōu was the last major stop in the rail line that branched out all over northern China. And now this key transport and railway hub was controlled by Féng Yùxiáng.

**07:37** That's why, in June 1927 both factions of the KMT, the Left and the Right, were actively courting Féng Yùxiáng, trying to win him over to their side. Negotiators from Wāng Jīngwèi and Chiang Kai-shek were holding secret meetings with Feng, making all kinds of promises and offering attractive cash bribes.

**08:00** And on June 19, 1927, two months after the Shanghai Massacre, Chiang Kai-shek had his turn to personally meet face to face with Féng Yùxiáng. Their first encounter. Féng had just left a meeting the other day with Wāng Jīngwèi's people to see what they had to offer him. And now it was time to see what promises and financial incentives Chiang and the KMT Right would make. Whoever offered the best deal, that's who Féng Yùxiáng went with. Basic Warlord Theory 101.

**08:32** There's a story about how when Chiang Kai-shek went up to Xúzhōu, Jiangsu province, waiting for the Christian Warlord, Féng's train pulled up and he walked out of a box car dressed like a common soldier and announced himself to a very surprised Chiang, who was expecting someone a little more professional and dignified looking. This was later called a big setup and that Féng had actually rode in more comfortably appointed rooms and that before the train got to the station in Xúzhōu, Féng switched train cars and changed into more humble soldier's garb. He carried out the same ruse with Wāng Jīngwèi, I read.

**09:11** Féng Yùxiáng had grown disillusioned with the Soviets after his short stint there following the Anti-Fèngtiān War and had enough sense of patriotism to see what they had in mind as far as which direction they'd like to see China go. So that's one reason he ended up shaking hands with Chiang Kai-shek at this meeting. And the Generalissimo saw to it that after they had both come to a general understanding, a two million dollar per month cherry on top of everything else was promised.

Chiang Kai-shek, the closer. So Féng Yùxiáng, this time around, in June 1927 was going to fight on the side of the Nationalists.

09:53 And he made his intentions known in the form of a telegram sent to the Wǔhàn government in which he suggested three things. First, get rid of all the communists and Soviet advisers. Second was to go join the Nanjing government and lastly, he suggested some leaders in the faction go take a nice extended European vacation. And that, my friends, was pretty much the end of the Wǔhàn Left-leaning KMT government. The Soviets knew the jig was up and packed up and started heading home. And Wāng Jīngwèi took the Betraying General up on that European holiday idea.

10:33 And once he declared his loyalties to Chiang and the NRA, Féng Yùxiáng carried out a purge in his own ranks too, of all communists. This included his illustrious political commissar at the time, Mr. Dèng Xiǎopíng. He had to make a quick exit. And not long after, Deng will run into Máo Zédōng in Wǔhàn, his first meeting with the future Great Helmsman. We all know what happens after that, also mentioned so many times in past episodes. Communist operatives everywhere throughout 1927 and into 1928 were hunted down and killed or driven underground until it was safe to come out.

11:14 The KMT and the two armies controlled by the Wǔhàn faction and the Nánjīng faction couldn't fight as one. Too much bad blood out there. And consequently Zhāng Zuòlín and his forces, led primarily by the Dogmeat

THE
CHP
CHINA HISTORY PODCAST
THE TRANSCRIPTS

THE WARLORD ERA
PART 9

General Zhāng Zōngchāng and the Nanking Warlord Sūn Chuánfāng, fought hard and took back all the territory they had lost to the NRA during the summer of 1927. And after suffering a major drubbing at the hands of Sūn Chuánfāng's forces around Nanjing, Chiang Kai-shek was back on his heels.

**11:52** A poor result on the battlefield and getting outmaneuvered by his fellow rivals in the KMT forced Chiang in August 1927 to step down and he removed himself from the action. It had been four months since the Shanghai Massacre and the blowback from that and Chiang's inability to finish off the Northern Expedition caused Chiang to make a political tactical withdrawal.

**12:20** It ended up taking the combined efforts of Lǐ Zōngrén, Hé Yìngqīn and Féng Yùxiáng's armies to finally defeat Sūn Chuánfāng in September 1927. This allowed NRA troops to catch somewhat of a breather with Sun out of the way. That had been an exhausting string of battles. He had been a menace to not only his enemies but society as well, all throughout 1925-26 and 27. His troops saw a lot of action and wherever there was action, innocent civilians lost their lives or had them turned upside down.

**12:59** So, August 1927 Chiang Kai-shek retreated to his hometown of Xīkǒu where he began a self-imposed five-month exile. Xīkǒu is located just a little southwest of Níngbō which is why Chiang Kai-shek is considered a Níngbō rén, And there, in Xīkǒu, Chiang waited things out.

**13:21** If you ever find yourself in Níngbō with nothing to do, go visit this place. Quite historic. Xīkǒu is where Chiang stashed Zhāng Xuéliáng after the Xīān Incident in 1936. The villa he shared with Sòng Měilíng is also there in Xīkǒu, the Měilíng Gōng.

**13:40** And speaking of Sòng Měilíng, as this drama is all playing out, Chiang in the summer of 1927, asked for her hand in marriage and this time she accepted. Back in 1922 when he met her at a party at Sun Yat-sen's house, he was a relative nobody compared to someone the likes of Sòng Měilíng. But not anymore. In 1922 she looked down on him as too common and rough around the edges. But now, despite the political circumstances of the moment, he was arguably the leading military and political figure at a time when there were a lot of powerful military and political figures operating on the stage of Chinese history. So, what wasn't such a great catch five years ago all the sudden wasn't looking so bad. Hitching her carriage to Chiang Kai-shek wasn't a bad deal for Sòng Měilíng, nor for the whole Sòng Family clan. And for Chiang, I might add.

**14:40** And if you remember from that old Whitey Smith episode CHP-193, on December 1, 1927 forty year-old Chiang Kai-shek and twenty-six year old Sòng Měilíng were wed. And that most gala event of the year was held that same evening in the Majestic Hotel with Whitey in all his glory, the great showman, up on the bandstand. What a night.

15:05 | By the end of 1927, things within the KMT were sufficiently in enough disarray that it was felt in some circles that maybe bringing back Chiang wasn't such a bad idea. And so on January 1st, 1928, with the KMT now unified, or more unified than usual, Chiang Kai-shek was handed the leadership of the Party. And then on February 18, he was made commander-in-chief of the Northern Expeditionary forces with Hé Yìngqīn serving as his deputy.

15:35 | This second phase of the Northern Expedition that had languished for almost a year was going to once and for all bring down Zhāng Zuòlín. That was the plan anyway. To do this, four armies were organized. The First Army, or Central Army, based in Nanjing, they were led by Chiang and were chock-full of Whampoa Military Academy officer and soldiers. The Second Army was essentially Féng Yùxiáng's Guómínjūn or National People's Army. The Third was the army of the Shānxī Warlord, Yán Xíshān. And the Fourth Army was led by Lǐ Zōngrén and his Guǎngxī Army. Warlords fighting warlords. What else was new? On Chiang's side all warlord armies combined had about seven hundred thousand troops fighting against about four hundred thousand warlord troops on the other side.

16:33 | And so, on April 9, 1928, almost a year to the day that Chiang kicked the hornets nest and unleashed the Shanghai Massacre and White Terror, The Northern Expedition was launched again. Last time, the Japanese Guāndōng Army stopped him before the NRA was able to march into Shandong. He was planning to do it now whether they liked it or not. And his army headed in the direction of Shandong, the land of the two great and ancient states of Qí and Lǔ. Chiang Kai-shek knew, there was gonna be some kind of reaction from Japan. Let's wait and see.

17:13 And over in Shānxī province the Model Governor, Yán Xīshān, leading his own army, the third of the four Northern Expedition armies... he had decided it was best for him to have moved his chips over to the Chiang Kai-shek side. All this time, Zhāng Zuòlín had been making overtures to Yán Xīshān to have him declare his loyalties to the Fèngtiān side. As Yán Xīshān always did, he weighed his options, considered the merits and benefits and decided on what was best for him. And what was best for Yán Xīshān, at least while he was in charge, was always best for Shānxī Province.

17:53 So with Chiang's army on the march heading in the direction of the Shandong capital, the Japanese officials in Jìnán called their big strong buddies in the Guāndōng Army and said something's about to go down and it won't be good for Team Japan. The two thousand or so Japanese nationals in Jinan were gonna need some protection. So they told the Guāndōng Army they better send about three thousand troops or so.

18:20 Only a few weeks into the re-launch of the Northern Expedition, the First and Second Armies were camped outside of Jinan. Chiang Kai-shek showed up in early May 1928 and at once started negotiating with the Japanese to persuade them to leave Jinan and allow the NRA to come in and reestablish political and administrative control over the city.

18:43 You know, it worked in ancient times. If you set your mind to something, all you need is an incident to point to to justify some extreme action that you're looking to take.

18:55 And just as Chiang thought taking back Jinan was going to be easy. What followed Chiang's attempted takeover of Jinan is written into the Chinese history books as the Jinan Incident. The Wǔsān Cǎn'àn, May Third 1928. It worked so well for Japan they did it again on JiǔYīBā, 9-18-1931. In trying to gingerly establish control of the city, a bunch of Japanese got roughed up, a couple dozen or so killed. Before you could say *casus belli*, the Japanese military on May 8, 1928 launched an all-out attack on the city of Jinan. Five thousand Chinese killed. It was a romp. Japan then held Jinan close to their chest until they were forced to let go in March 1929.

19:48 Not surprisingly, and you can dig deeper if you want to, like a lot of these incidents that happened in China, between the Japanese and Chinese, the CCP and KMT, the CCP and the USA and so on and so forth whoever had a horse in that race, there's always more than one version supported by the different groups involved. In any case, Chiang Kai-shek cut his losses and moved on to the big prize, the final destination, the zhōngdiǎnzhàn of the campaign, the last stop, the city of Beijing, where Zhāng Zuòlín awaited.

**20:23** But as Chiang's diaries reveal, and he was most prolific about recording his thoughts in his private diaries, from here on out, he will know China's greatest enemy without was Japan and they could never be trusted. His attitudes toward Japan were very much impacted by the outcome of this Jinan Incident. He never forgot it. And not just Chiang. The whole military establishment didn't need to have the outcome explained to them. And Chinese civilians who knew what was going on, their attitudes towards Japan hardened as well.

**21:00** The Northern Expedition combined forces, began pushing the Dogmeat General Zhāng Zōngchāng and the Young Marshal Zhāng Xuéliáng back north to their particular strongholds. As for Wú Pèifú, fighting on Zhāng Zuòlín's side against the NRA, he too could not hold back the Chiang's and decided to retreat to Sichuan province and finally get out of the warlord business. Zhāng Zōngchāng was soundly defeated and went back to his home province of Shandong, the very province that he had ruled as his own personal kingdom and cash cow. He's going to make a grab to get back to those glory days but we'll look at that next episode.

**21:42** The Japanese liked everything just the way it was in Manchuria with Zhang Zuolin in charge of matters. The Old Marshal didn't see eye to eye on everything with the Japanese, but with him in charge they were given a rather free hand to go kick the tires all over north China and shop for some new acquisitions.

**22:01** The Mukden Incident was still four years away and the Marco Polo Bridge Incident a decade away. But by the late 1920s, the anti-Japanese feeling all over China was very palpable. Incidents happened all the time. Japanese nationals often got hurt or roughed up by the locals. And now Japanese troops and weapons were pouring into China under the pretense of protecting Japanese citizens and interests in China. More and more Japanese naval vessels were plying China's coast and great rivers.

**22:37** And because he didn't do anything about this as it was happening before everyone's eyes, Chiang Kai-shek ended up getting heaps of criticism from every corner for putting up with Japanese arrogance and aggression and not taking the fight to them when they were so disrespecting China. He appeased the Japanese too easily, his critics said. Chiang secretly knew after these warlords were dealt with once and for all, he'd have to deal with Japan next in one form or another. He didn't want to take on both at the same time.

**23:11** By May 1928 Chiang's 1st and 2nd Armies were advancing on Beijing. Zhāng Zuòlín was still in control of the capital, but he knew things weren't looking good. Former frenemy Yan Xishan was advancing from the west, now fighting on Chiang's side against him. The Old Marshal had read his Sūnzǐ as well as anyone, and he knew when the right time was to take a tactical retreat. Two months into the campaign, the NRA had taken Beijing.

22:41 | And Zhāng Zuòlín did something that he didn't do too often. When Japan had threatened everyone to keep their fighting out of Manchuria or else, the Old Marshal didn't like that and told them where to stick that. Something about Zhāng Zuòlín, the Japanese were starting to have second thoughts about how pliable their old friend was going to be as far as bending to their demands.

24:05 | June 3, 1928, Zhāng Zuòlín along with his entourage boarded his private train, pulled out of Beijing station and headed in the direction of Shěnyáng. Then in the early hours of the morning of June 4, 1928, just as his train was approaching northwest Shenyang at Huánggūtún Station, bombs were set off on a bridge that Zhāng Zuòlín's train carriage was passing under. It collapsed and killed the Manchurian Warlord. Not instantly, but he perished before lunchtime. This was known as the Huánggūtún Shìjiàn. The Huánggūtún Incident.

24:46 | Blowing up Zhāng Zuòlín's train was an utter and complete disaster for Japan and was terribly bungled by rogue elements inside the Guāndōng Army who took it upon themselves to deal drastically with this Manchurian Warlord who was mouthing off to them. Talking to the Soviets. Talking to the Americans.

25:06 | The conspirators meant for this to be the Mukden Incident that would create the wherewithal for Japan to take over Manchuria. But instead, right at the outset, things didn't go according to plan. It failed in its main objective. Even Emperor Hirohito gave the ones responsible a written tongue lashing. The hawks in the

Guandong Army had to wait till 9-18-1931 to finally get their Mukden Incident.

26:35    And the upshot to all this, that perhaps most of all contributed to making this a disaster for Japan in Manchuria, was that Zhāng Xuéliáng on June 19, 1928 called Chiang Kai-shek and lets him know he too was joining the NRA side. The Japanese bumped off the Old Marshal because he was dragging his heels on a lot of what the Guāndōng military was asking for. They wrongly predicted that Zhāng Zuòlín's drug addict playboy son, the Young Marshal, Zhang Xueliang, would be a less pugnacious warlord to deal with.

26:12    But they misjudged him. Zhāng Xuéliáng didn't require too many brain cells to see what Japan's Guāndōng Army was up to. And he knew he didn't have enough muscle power to take Japan on alone. But the Young Marshal knew he could really throw a wrench in their plans by joining up with the Nationalist government and throwing his lot in with Chiang Kai-shek. Watching Zhang Xueliang army raise the Nationalist flag in Manchuria was just about the last thing Japan wanted to see happen. Should have thought twice before they went and blowed up Zhāng Zuòlín's train. This was a stunning reversal of fortune for Japan.

26:50    So with Zhāng Zuòlín out of the way and Zhāng Xuéliáng now on his side, Chiang Kai-shek's army took Beijing on July 6, 1928. And that was the official end of the Northern Expedition. Or was it? We'll see what happened next in the conclusion of this Warlord series.

27:10 | That's gonna be it for this time ladies and gentlemans. Laszlo Montgomery signing off from Los Angeles, California hoping and praying you'll find it in your heart to come back one more time for another exciting episode of The China History Podcast, not to mention the conclusion to this series. Take care everyone.

# The Warlord Era
# Part 10

**THE TRANSCRIPTS**

## SUMMARY

In this concluding episode, we close the book on this China Warlord Era overview that began in 1916 and lingered on and on until 1930. By the time it was over Japan was on the cusp of their invasion of Manchuria, plunging China into another national crisis. We'll look at Zhang Zongchang's Warlord Rebellion in Northeast Shandong as well as Liu Zhennian, the Red Spears, and the Central Plains War.

## TRANSCRIPT

00:00 | Welcome back again everyone. Thanks for tuning in to the concluding episode of this ten part series that examined the big picture of this terrible Warlord Era. As I said at the outset, this was an oft requested topic here at the China History Podcast. These warlords have always been a subject of great interest in popular Chinese history. There were a lot of historical events happening in China during the 20th century. These years from 1916 to 1928 are often swept under the rug and don't get as much attention. So I hope this series helped to fill in a few blanks for you.

00:40 | And as we have seen throughout the past episodes, these warlords weren't such a great bunch of guys. Interesting, yes. In some cases, downright unforgettable.

00:51 | I've introduced a number of them to you and tried to show you how they operated and what some of them were all about. They made incalculable contributions to the art of greed and looking out for number one. Took it to great heights.

01:05 | In all the thousands of years of Chinese history going back to Yǔ the Great, the land had time and again produced these incredible leaders and heroes who founded dynasties, saved the country from invasion or brought great peace and prosperity to the land. But during the 1920s, rather than having a great leader and nation builder waiting in the wings to, I don't know, make China great again, instead you had these warlords. And with their armies and the might they wielded and the odious and egregious lengths they went to, to enrich themselves and guard their power for the sake of the perks of power and all the human suffering they caused, their greatest crime was perhaps that they held China back at the historical worst possible moment.

01:57 | While Japan and the West were setting the world on fire with all the discoveries and benefits of the Industrial Revolution and the engineering innovations of the roaring twenties, China wasted decades, first dealing with a dysfunctional and dying imperial house, and then with these generals and majors, out in a world of their own, dragging the country down, not to mention the good people of China too.

02:23 | After the Northern Expedition officially ended in the summer of 1928 and Beijing had been taken, all the victorious generals had their great moment. And then Chiang Kai-shek called a meeting of all the big names at the time, and he held it over in the Western Hills, just outside of Beijing. Féng Yùxiáng, Yán Xīshān, Bái Chóngxǐ, Lǐ Zōngrén and others. There was this big ceremony where they all visited Sun Yat-sen's tomb. It was still up in Beijing at this time. And they paid their respects to the spiritual founder of the KMT.

02:58     Now, Chiang will later have an elaborate mausoleum built in Nanjing and it's there where the Father of Modern China was later interred and remains today. If you remember from that old Morris "Two-Gun" Cohen episode CHP-130 and 131, Moishe was part of that cortege that brought Sun's body to its final resting place in Nanjing. And by the way, Moish didn't do too bad in the arms business during the Warlord Era. And some of you may or may not recall Sir Edmund Backhouse? Yeah, he too dabbled in the arms biz.

03:33     During this conference in the Western Hills with all his allies Chiang laid out his master plan and discussed the matter of demilitarization and centralizing everything.

03:45     Although nobody got up and walked out of the meeting, it wasn't received very well by any of these men present. The whole idea about surrendering their power over the regions they controlled for the sake of a strong central government? They didn't like that idea in 1916 and they didn't like it in 1928 either. And when they saw what Chiang's plan looked like, these warlords began to have

THE
CHP
CHINA HISTORY PODCAST
THE TRANSCRIPTS

THE WARLORD ERA
PART 10

second thoughts, again. But for now, no one was saying or doing anything.

04:18   It was always the same thing. They were cool with being part of the Republic of China. They just insisted that they be left alone by the center to run their province and maintain an army. That's what it boiled down to. Eastern Zhōu Dynasty mentality, I guess you can say. Like Duke Huán of Qí back in the 7th century BCE, he was happy to say yeah, yeah, yeah to the Zhōu King in Luòyáng, as long as that king didn't try and interfere in Qí internal affairs. Same with these warlords and Chiang Kai-shek and his Nanjing government. In their eyes, these warlords looked at Chiang Kai-shek and thought he was just another one of them. Why should they surrender their power to him?

05:00   Chiang's sad reality was that he was only the master of the Yangzi river region from Wǔhàn to Shanghai, in Jiāngsū, and Zhèjiāng and parts of Shāndōng province. That's it. Everywhere else in China? Like I said, Eastern Zhōu Dynasty.

05:16   Before we start looking at the events of 1929 and 1930, let's take a step back and talk about something else pretty important that concerned the warlords that's been going on in the background around the time of the Northern Expedition. I sort of left you hanging about what ever happened to the Dogmeat General, Zhāng Zōngchāng. This whole sidebar to the Warlord Era that I want to quickly mention concerned him and his former right-hand man in his military organization Liú Zhēnnián, a.k.a. "The Killer." So you know right away he's no Yán Xīshān.

**05:51** During his glory years running Shāndōng province, Zhāng Zōngchāng had two main guys watching his back. Chǔ Yùpú and Liú Zhènnián. As warlords went, as far as the superlative of the worst elements that warlords embodied, these three set the standard. Thanks to them, Shāndōng province had a hard decade and a half.

**06:15** They epitomized all the most well-known warlord antics that peasants had become accustomed to all these years, standing by helpless while warlords troops grabbed what they could, using all the intimidation tactics that an army at your beck and call can muster.

**06:32** Villagers, especially those in Shāndōng province where all three of these guys operated, were made to hand over food, anything of value, including their pack animals. To escape the worst of the looting villages and towns would be "asked," quotation marks around the word asked to pay a 'departure tax' that would spare them the worst atrocities and allow the troops to go quietly. And same thing when these bandit forces would march into a village or town. They'd demand a kind of 'welcome payment' that would guarantee the locals there wouldn't be trouble with them passing through or staying around to rest up and live off their hospitality. Everything about these guys always came down to money. And those who had the least were forced to hand over the most.

**07:23** And when famines, floods and other natural disasters hit, you can be sure whatever relief supplies donated by the city folk or from overseas, that stuff often would miss its mark and get plundered and sold on the black market. Banks were forced to extend loans to these warlords that they knew would never be repaid. After so many years, the warlords simply became a cost of doing business. Anyone or any organization that was well-endowed financially were targeted by warlords and forced to buy these worthless bonds that their military government would issue. I already mentioned warlords were big proponents of printing worthless money in these outrageous denominations. People from the top to the bottom of society were constantly being shaken down by warlords and their subordinates.

**08:13** They levied taxes on so many daily use items, and even on prostitutes. In many places there were dozens and even hundreds of different taxes on seemingly every product or service that you could tax. And if this wasn't bad enough, sometimes, to accelerate the amount of taxes that could be farmed, warlords would demand taxes be paid years in advance and they'd even be applied retroactively.

**08:38** And the great Chinese national hero Lín Zéxú who stood up to the foreign powers in 1839, if he had lived to see how huge of a comeback opium had made and what a cash cow it had become again, he would have bowed his head in shame. Opium monopolies to market the drug in certain areas were sold off. And you can bet these warlords levied taxes on production, transport, the sale and the use of opium. It was a huge money spinner, as the drug trade always is.

09:11   If you recall, Zhāng Zōngchāng's army got walloped in the Northern Expedition and got taken down more than a few notches. This was due in great part to the defection of his now former right-hand man, Liú Zhēnnián to the NRA side. Yeah, he was another one, biting the hand that fed him.

09:30   Well, after getting chased out of Shāndōng, Zhāng Zōngchāng ultimately ended up in Dalian and pretty much got high all day, gambled and engaged in all the excesses he was well known for. And what was left of his army, though still loyal to Zhāng Zōngchāng, let's just say they got a little flabby and undisciplined as they awaited their boss's comeback.

09:52   Liú Zhēnnián, "The Killer," had profited greatly from his defection in October 1928 to Chiang Kai-shek's side. He got put in charge of a portion of eastern Shāndōng province. What's important to know is that life under Liú Zhēnnián's rule in Eastern Shāndōng was shockingly unpleasant. I've already given you an idea of the kinds of things that went on. Almost as soon as Liú Zhēnnián took over, the people began rising up against him and kept him very preoccupied dealing with all these tempests in a teapot boiling over everywhere.

10:28   So in early 1929, Zhāng Zōngchāng, seeing how Liú was distracted with all these uprisings, and also, itching to restore his fortunes, started stirring things up in

Shāndōng province in his determination to bring Liú Zhēnnián down. He cobbled together a rebel army of former troops and other men without a master looking to get back into the game. And this Dogmeat General launched this rebellion in northeast Shāndōng against Liú Zhēnnián. Not much to say except that it didn't last long. January to May 1929. But the kind of things that went on, the kinds of things the civilian population had to endure, gave the Rape of Nanking a run for its money in terms of wanton violence and destruction.

11:16    Zhāng Zōngchāng famously, while all this fighting was going on, was constantly partying and living the life for which he had become accustomed. He was the head of the rebels but always found time to have some fun and relaxation. Liú Zhēnnián, despite his troops best efforts, by April 1929, this back-stabbing former right hand man of the Dogmeat General was losing a few key battles and on the defensive. All Zhang Zongchang's army had to do now was go in for the kill.

11:48    Maybe after smoking too much opium, who knows, the General "Carne de Perro", Zhang Zongchang, he dreamed up this "League of Legends" who he tried to bring together at this hour to take out the KMT. His remaining trusty right hand man Chǔ Yùpú as well as Yán Xīshān, Wú Pèifú, Bái Chóngxǐ, Qí Xièyuán and others were called upon to unite as one in this common cause. Needless to say, the reason why you probably might not recall anything happening involving all this warlord supergroup is because this whole idea fizzled out before anything came of it. But this was the kind of madness going on in mid-1929. And I haven't even gotten to the Central Plains War that's also going on. Let's finish this up first.

**12:38** As soon as Zhāng Zōngchāng got a taste of victory in this rebellion against Liú Zhēnnián, his troops just fell to pieces and discipline broke down to the point where his forces, the other rebel soldiers and officers, everyone, the whole thing just devolved into another classic free-for-all with all these soldiers and bandits preying on the lives of every villager they came upon in every single nook and cranny of the northeast Shāndōng countryside.

**13:07** You know, if you go to Manchuria, Liáoníng mostly, but Hēilóngjiāng and Jílín as well, there are a lot of people living there who came from Shāndōng. And it was during this Warlord Rebellion in northeastern Shāndōng, during the first half of 1929, that so many of them migrated north to Manchuria.

**13:28** Zhāng Zōngchāng, after looking like he was gonna make that comeback, faced a complete route on the battlefield, and whatever he had managed to hold together was lost. He tried to escape to Dalian on April 23, 1929 but the Japanese wouldn't let him stay. He got sent off to Japan. We'll get back to him later. And whilst cooling his heels in Japan after this failed uprising, he one day accidentally shot some prince who was a cousin to the deposed Last Emperor Pǔyí. That clan was a very interesting royal family in exile.

14:05    Anyways, by the summer 1929 Liú Zhēnnián started mopping up from the defeat he had handed to all these rebel allies of the Dogmeat General.

14:13    But during the second half of 1929, Liú Zhēnnián focused all of his attention on wiping out this other problem that had been dogging him all along while he was trying to vanquish Zhāng Zōngchāng and his rebel armies. These were the Red Spears. A very interesting story from Chinese history. Lots of legends and tales about these guys. These Red Spears had been harassing the warlord armies for too many years and had become very emboldened with their actions. Their numbers were as high as fifty to sixty thousand trained and fearless troops.

14:51    The Red Spears Society, the Hóng Qiāng Huì, they came about as a result of the lawlessness throughout the provinces. Some places were worse than others, of course. But the peasantry living out in the villages, especially during these years when Zhāng Zōngchāng, Chǔ Yùpú and Liú Zhēnnián were robbing and a stabbing, looting and a shooting and plundering the land, their troops, as well as these roaming gangs of bandits, ex-soldiers who departed their units and other assorted ruffians, they had developed a good eye for a hot meal and a village to ransack.

15:27    To defend against these bandit gangs, these villages, in an age old tradition in Chinese history, would pool their resources and maintain these rural defense organizations who would be just big and scary enough to keep these roving bandit gangs moving on to easier meat elsewhere.

**15:46** And in that part of China they became known as Red Spears. Some were less ragtag than others and were well-organized and could inflict some heavy damage when the times called for that. They mostly operated out of the provinces of Hubei, Henan and Shāndōng as well as in Manchuria. And for the entire time from the establishment of Manchukuo in 1932 until Japan's end in China came in 1945, these Red Spears were a snake in the boot to the Japanese Guāndōng Army and resisted them whenever the opportunity presented itself.

**16:22** It was this horrible and bloody period of intra-warlord fighting in Shandong that forced so many peasants to join the ranks of the Red Spears. Probably the worst of these uprisings happened in northeast Shandong from 1928 to 1929 when these events I've just described were all happening.

**16:41** Let me quote from Elizabeth J. Perry's book *Rebels and Revolutionaries in North China 1845-1945*: "Like the Boxers, the Red Spears evidenced a heavy dose of popular religious inspiration, members believing themselves impervious to enemy weapons if they observed the necessary rituals, pronounced the proper incantations, and swallowed the prescribed charms. And, again resembling the Boxers, the Red Spears were heirs to another equally vital legacy: the militia tradition of rural self-defense."

**17:16** When the chaos of the early Republican era reached a fever pitch after the fall of the Qīng dynasty, the people of north China especially had to put up with almost twenty years of getting jacked by all these bandits and soldiers from warlord armies, which in a lot of cases were one and the same.

**17:35** So the Red Spears initially came into being as protectors of the countryside. Not every village could be defended. There were too many spread out across Shandong, Hebei and Henan where the worst of the atrocities were committed.

**17:48** There were a number of large and small uprisings involving the Red Spears fighting back against the twin terrors of Shandong province. First, the Dogmeat General in 1926 and then again in 1928-1929 against The Killer, Liú Zhēnnián.

**18:06** In a 1926 issue of Chinese Students Monthly, someone wrote of these defenders of the oppressed: "These Boxers call themselves 'Red Spears.' While the object of the previous uprising was purely anti-foreign, the Red Spears is a spontaneous peasants movement. The name of Red Spear Society must have existed five to six years ago. There was a group of gymnastic people who had the useful and necessary habit of defending themselves and their villages by long and red tasseled spears. As an institution it may be just the remnant of the Boxers."

**18:45** You know, if you Google Red Spears and martial arts, there are all kinds of stories, legends, and styles that grew out of their society, especially in training and hand to hand combat. And they used these martial arts skills that they developed to defend their villages, homes and livelihoods against this never-ending scourge of banditry and lawlessness.

**19:09** By early 1929, the excesses of Liú Zhēnnián's rule were so oppressive that the Red Spears directed their efforts to bringing him down. It all started with mutinies within Liú Zhēnnián's ranks late in January 1929 just as Zhang Zongchang was starting the rebellion up in the northeast of Shāndōng. A lot of these mutinied soldiers and officers joined with the Red Spears against Liú Zhēnnián, who again had his hands full dealing with this Warlord Rebellion in northeast Shāndōng. The Red Spears used this chaos as a way to organize and grow their numbers. But as I said, end April 1929, despite having the upper hand, Zhāng Zōngchāng was defeated and this allowed Liú's armies to focus their attention on problem number two.

**20:00** I won't drag this out. Basically, as big and tough as the Red Spears were, in the end, Liú Zhēnnián packed a mean punch. They didn't call him "The Killer" for nothing. Jerry Lee Lewis too. Liú had a formidable army, the best weapons and was more than happy to carry out a scorched earth policy all over the parts of Shāndōng his troops marched in his relentless mission to snuff out every possible Red Spear base around Yāntái and other parts of the province. And before the end of the year 1929, the job was done and the Red Spears had been neutralized. But their legend lived on.

**20:40** Let's get back to where we left off with Chiang Kai-shek. Things appeared okay on the surface in the weeks and months following the raising of the Nationalist flag in Beijing, or Běipíng as it was re-named following the conquest. End 1928, I told you we already know who's grumbling behind Chiang's back.

**21:01** On the symbolic day of October 10th, this time in the year 1928, Chiang Kai-shek was formally named the head of the Republic. He was also the top man in the Party and the commander-in-chief of the military. Not as many titles as the current president of China but still, he was at the peak of his prestige and power on the Chinese mainland. The Nánjīng Decade was off and running.

**21:26** As 1929 dawned it came time for action. Chiang had made it clear what his intentions were. Now it was time to show your cards. Chiang intended to fold all these warlords and their armies and assets into this new centralized military force, with Chiang in charge of course. And a few of these warlords, as I mentioned, began to have buyer's remorse when considering this new life they had to look forward to, punching a clock for someone else versus having the absolute power they enjoyed all these years being the dūjūn or military governor of their province or territory.

**22:07** To give them a little face and draw them into the government, Chiang had made Yán Xīshān his Minister of the Interior and Féng Yùxiáng, Minister of War. Not bad except, after the life they had lived, those two were bored with their jobs in two seconds flat. You know,

Chiang Kai-shek didn't give a speech in front of a big sign that said "Mission Accomplished" but it seemed as far as the Northern Expedition went, that it was over. But alas, this miserable and destructive epoch refused to die and go away.

**22:42** All these former warlords, they all basically bolted from Chiang's Nánjīng government and went back into the warlording business, of protecting their turf, farming their provinces for all they could get, keeping the central authorities at bay, and always keeping an eye out for any kind of opportunity that knocked on their door.

**23:04** Féng Yùxiáng went back to controlling his parts of Inner Mongolia, Gānsù, Shǎnxī and Hénán. Yán Xīshān of course held down the fort in his home province of Shānxī. The Young Marshal Zhāng Xuéliáng, he too, for the time being, had given up on Chiang and was disappointed with Chiang's plans for Manchuria. But he remained neutral and waited on the fence to see how this played out. And as for the Guǎngxī warlords who had served Chiang so well, Lǐ Zōngrén and Bái Chóngxǐ, they were the first ones to walk away from him in March 1929. And they headed back to their strongholds in Guǎngdōng and Guǎngxī.

**23:46** And with all this resistance to Chiang Kai-shek wafting in the air, Wāng Jīngwèi saw an opening to get back into the fray. So he returned to China and joined up with Féng Yùxiáng and Yán Xīshān in a rival political group called the "Enlarged Conference of the KMT".

24:04 So Chiang once again had to waste precious time that could have been more productively spent trying to get his Nánjīng government up and running, carrying out the massive reconstruction of the country, and try to rebuild the nation to its former glory before the Qing emperors and Republican era warlords allowed it to decay.

24:26 It seemed like it was going to come down to one last and final hurrah, and this was the Central Plains War of March 1929 to November 1930. And of all the wars I've mentioned going back to the Zhílì-Ānhuī War when the forces of Cáo Kūn and Wú Pèifú defeated Duàn Qíruì's Ānhuī Army back in 1920, this one was the most destructive. In the thousands of years of Chinese history these lands had never seen anything like this. And there was still a lot worse to come over the next couple decades.

25:03 Now here we are at the end of 1929, so many years later, and these warlords, the ones left standing, they were making this last-ditch effort to hold on to what they had gotten used to all these years.

25:17 And everything I mentioned about the Warlord Rebellion in northeast Shandong and the rise and fall of the Red Spears... that was all going on concurrently to this. Early 1929, the warlord rebellion was over and late 1929, Liú Zhēnnián had put the Red Spears to the sword.

25:34 And one other thing, we'll come back and look at this more closely on another day, but right around this time, Chiang also set up his very effective secret police organization. His old pal from the Whampoa Military Academy Dài Lì, The Himmler of China, was called in to head up the Army's secret police and Chén Lìfū, he was put in charge of the innocuous sounding Investigation Section of the KMT Organization Department. You didn't want those guys knocking on your door after hours. Much more about these two guys later in the year. I know several of you have written to me over the years asking when Dài Lì was going to get his CHP moment.

26:15   Anyways, in November 1929 Féng Yùxiáng led the charge and formed a warlord coalition to oppose Chiang Kai-shek, who everyone knew was coming after them. And the eternal foe of Chiang Kai-shek, Wāng Jīngwèi, now part of this group, tried to resurrect the KMT Left Wing and form a band called "The Reorganizationalists" who's goal was to put an end to Chiang Kai-shek's so-called dictatorial ways.

26:46   And these Leftists and Warlords all banded together and formed a rival government in Beijing to oppose Chiang's government based in Nánjīng. And the one who was made the figurehead leader of this rival government was good old Yán Xīshān. The Model Governor wasn't happy with Chiang moving in on his turf so he ended up joining the anti-Chiang coalition.

27:10   I mentioned Yán Xīshān graced the cover of Time in 1930 with the caption "China's Future President." Hah, this was that time. That cover ended up being a precursor to "Dewey Defeats Truman."

179

27:24  So who stuck with Chiang and fought on his side? For one, and I haven't mentioned them much, were the warlords who ran Western China, all Muslims, all members of the Mǎ Clique.

27:35  When hostilities had broken out in March 1929, on paper at least, with so many warlords teamed up against him, it wasn't looking good for Chiang or the Nanjing government. But a combination of good luck and bad coordination on the warlord coalition's part helped turn the tide of the Central Plains War in favor of the NRA.

27:59  By the summer of 1930, Chiang began fighting back and his generals performed well against the Guǎngxī warlords Lǐ Zōngrén and Bái Chóngxǐ. Féng Yùxiáng too, up in his north China lands, went down in defeat. Then on September 18th, 1930, Zhāng Xuéliáng hopped down off that fence and entered the war on Chiang's side. Following this, he immediately went in and took Beijing. And with Zhāng Xuéliáng entering the war on Chiang's side, that ended up tipping the scales sufficiently enough so that on November 4th, Féng Yùxiáng and Yán Xīshān both threw in the towel.

28:40  They had tried one last time to keep the warlord era going. But by November 1930, it really was over. The Central Plains War pretty much ended it.

28:53  This whole Central Plains War, the upshot of it all, aside from finally putting an end to the most offending warlords, it forced Chiang Kai-shek to take his eye off the ball in his campaigns to destroy Máo Zédōng and the Jiāngxī Soviet that he was preparing to setup in 1931. While Chiang was battling it out with the warlords in the Central Plains War, the Communists had ample time to reenergize and get reorganized for all the trials and tribulations that lay ahead.

**29:25** Anyways, I knew this episode was gonna run a little long and we sort of glossed over a conflict that from March 1929 to November 1930 resulted in the deaths of about 150,000 Nationalist soldiers, and though we can never be certain, probably just as many on the warlord side.

**29:44** And whatever happened to all these guys? These rascals? These permanent members of China History's Rogue's Gallery?

**29:55** Duàn Qíruì, after his comeback as Chief Executive following the 2nd Zhílì Fèngtiān War from 1922-24, didn't have much of a base anymore. Most of his Ānhuī Clique allies had already thrown their lot in with Zhāng Zuòlín. Duàn ended up in Tiānjìn, living below the radar and died at the age of 71 in 1936 in Shànghǎi.

**30:20** Cáo Kūn? I left you hanging with him. After he got removed as president in Féng Yùxiáng's Běijīng Coup of 1924, he served two years under house arrest and then ended up in that great city of exiles, Tiānjìn, where he died in 1938, age 75. It didn't end well for Cáo Kūn, but at least he got to be president.

**30:43** Qí Xièyuán? He ended badly. This Zhílì stalwart, besides going down in defeat on the wrong side of the Central Plains War, he ended up being executed in 1946 for collaborating with the Japanese during the war.

**30:59** Zhāng Xuéliáng? Of course later on in December 1936, in one of the defining moments in his life, famously participated in the Xī'ān Incident involving the kidnapping of Chiang Kai-shek and everything that followed in the wake of that tragedy. He surrendered to Chiang after it was done and lived under house arrest for pretty much the rest of his life. He was taken to Taiwan in 1949 and lived a quiet life up in the north suburbs of Taipei.

**31:29** When Chiang Kai-shek passed away on April 5, 1975, Zhāng Xuéliáng was released from this symbolic house arrest. In 1993 he moved to Hawaii where he died in 2001 at the age of a hundred. Chairman Mao and Premier Zhou both tried to get the Young Marshal to come visit China. But, like many who left in '49, he never went back.

**31:55** Liú Zhēnnián, the wretched and violent warlord of eastern Shandong who caused so much suffering to the local populace? He ended up on Chiang's side, maybe the bad side. He got sent to Jiāngxī Province to join others who were trying to blast Máo Zédōng and the Communists out of Jǐnggāngshān. He wasn't too hot on the whole thing and ended up being executed in 1935 for refusing to obey Chiang's direct order. Quite a lot of violence and depravity condensed into the only thirty-seven years that The Killer walked this earth.

**32:30** Wú Pèifú? In an obituary about Wú Pèifú, Life Magazine called him "China's only honest warlord." He laid low until the Second Sino-Japanese War broke out in 1937. The Japanese had attempted to set up this rival government up in north China in 1939 and went to a lot of trouble to try and recruit Wú Pèifú as the puppet head of this government. He refused. And for his defiance the Japanese authorities, if you believe some accounts, had him poisoned to death. *The New York Times,* in their obituary of Wú Pèifú written on December 5, 1939 said it this way: "Marshal Wú Pèifú, Chinese poet-soldier died today after an operation for an infected tooth, the Japanese news agency Domei reported. Marshal Wú had lived in obscurity since his armies were routed in 1926 by Chiang Kai-shek. The Japanese had tried vainly to enlist his aid. Marshal Wú was one of the cultivated Chinese of our times who attained renown not only for his scholarship but as a military man." He lived to 65.

**33:44** And Sūn Chuánfāng? The Northern Expedition pretty much put him out of business. He ended up in Tianjin where he became a monk and lived in a monastery. Ten years after Sūn Chuánfāng executed one of his commanders, Shī Cóngbīn, and mounted his head on the end of a pike, the man's daughter, Shī Jiànqiào, caught up with the former Nanking Warlord in 1935 and avenged her father's death with a bullet to the brain for Sūn Chuánfāng. And this avenging daughter went on trial for murder. She received a government pardon and her act of vengeance was considered justified.

THE
**CHP**
CHINA HISTORY PODCAST
THE TRANSCRIPTS

THE WARLORD ERA
PART 10

34:21 | And Zhāng Zōngchāng, the good old Dogmeat General? Live by the sword, die by the sword. He too had it coming and he got it in 1932. Just like with Sūn Chuánfāng, an avenging angel came and smote him. For killing his father, the general Zhèng Jīnshēng in 1927, this son Zhèng Jìchéng caught up with the fifty year-old Dogmeat General and blew him away right at the Jǐnán train station.

34:49 | And Lǐ Zōngrén, the Guǎngxī Warlord... boy, did he ever have a wild ride after that whole debacle with the rival government up in Beijing in 1929 and surrendering to Chiang Kai-shek. He ended up in his stronghold of Guǎngxī and reconciled with Chiang after the Mukden Incident in 1931 when Japan invaded Manchuria and started taking over up there. He fought brilliantly against Japan during those terrible years in the late 1930's and early 40s. After Chiang bailed in 1949 and fled to Taiwan, the dubious honor of the presidency of the Republic of China on the mainland went to Lǐ Zōngrén. He ended up leaving as well but he went to the United States instead. Zhōu Ēnlái invited him back in 1965, which was a big deal back then. Li Zongren took him up on the offer and returned to China where he died in Beijing in 1969 at the age of 78.

35:47 | The Húnán Warlord, Táng Shēngzhì, he had a rough road. After breaking with Chiang and going his own way, he returned to the KMT fold to help in the war effort against the Japanese. And Táng Shēngzhì, if you recall from that past Nanjing Massacre two-part series, CHP-182-183, he was the one Chiang had put in charge of defending the capital of Nanjing. He didn't have a chance, and during that horrific week in the cold winter of December 1937, Táng Shēngzhì ended up being overwhelmed by the Japanese war machine and ordered a general retreat, leaving the city of Nanjing essentially undefended against the Japanese troops. He never lived that one down. The one who allowed the Rape of Nanjing to happen. There was nothing he could have done, but he had to wear that badge of shame a long time. He stayed behind in China after Liberation and died in Changsha, Hunan in 1970, aged 80.

**36:49**  Yán Xīshān, the Model Governor? After the Japanese started spreading out all over north China, he fought them at every turn. They also tried to recruit him to be part of some puppet position but he wouldn't have any of that. He fought the Japanese until he couldn't fight any more. He had even cooperated with the Communists for three years from 1936 to 1939 in fighting Japan. But he had second thoughts about cooperating with Mao and later turned against them and fought the Communists bitterly throughout the Civil War. After putting up a hell of a fight, his army was defeated in Tàiyuán in April 1949. For the next several desperate months, Yán Xīshān got stuck in Nanjing mediating between the feuding Chiang Kai-shek and Lǐ Zōngrén. That was a thankless task. And after he took that final flight to Taiwan, Yan Xishan lived a quiet life. Chiang had promised him the sky once they got to Taiwan. But in the end, Chiang sidelined Yán Xīshān and there was nothing to do for the Model Governor except live a quiet retirement writing books and no doubt looking back on quite a life. He died on May 24, 1960 in Taipei at the age of 76.

38:09 Féng Yùxiáng, don't wanna forget him. He was defeated in the Central Plains War and got into the criticizing Chiang Kai-shek business. He vociferously lambasted Chiang for not taking the fight to the Japanese aggressively enough. Féng did his part to stand up to Japan in his slice of northern China where he had traditionally held away. There was no love lost or trust between Féng and Chiang. And the Christian Warlord was no match for Chiang Kai-shek's political astuteness. He ended up holding a number of positions in Chiang's government while it was still on the mainland. After 1945 he ended up becoming a major critic of Chiang and sympathized more with the Communists. In any case, Féng Yùxiáng ended up dying mysteriously on board a vessel sailing on the Black Sea in 1948 that caught fire. You can visit his tomb today next time you find yourself in Jìnán. It's located not too far away near Tài Shān.

39:10 You know, all the way until the end came in October 1949, to be honest, Chiang never got rid of these guys. They were defanged following the Central Plains War but they were still around. Chiang didn't mess with them and they didn't mess with Chiang. In fact their mutual hatred of Communism was a kind of binding agent that allowed these disparate frenemies to have some semblance of a common cause. So if the Northern Expedition's goal was to unify China under one government, you can say it wasn't achieved. And in some ways, 1930 wasn't looking too terribly different from 1922.

**39:50** Okay, let us abruptly end things right here. I do hope everyone who had been asking me to cover this topic all these years left the table full and satisfied. I left out more than I left in. So if this period in China is of particular interest to you, there are plenty of books and videos out there for you to peruse should you want to take a deeper dive.

**40:13** Okay, new topic next time. A good one. Recommended by one of you beautiful people, my beloved listeners and fans of this China History Podcast. This is Laszlo Montgomery, signing off from Los Angeles, California calling on all good and decent people everywhere to please come back next time for another exciting episode of the China History Podcast.

# THE CHINESE WARLORD ERA
# LIST OF TERMS

| Pinyin/Term | Chinese | English/Meaning |
|---|---|---|
| Ān-Fú Club | 安福俱乐部 | Duàn Qíruǐ's political organization. The political wing of the Anhui Clique |
| Ānguójūn | 安国军 | The National Peace Army, More about them in Part 9 |
| Ānhuī | 安徽 | Province in Eastern China |
| Anhui Clique | 皖系 | Also called The An-Fu Clique. One of the cliques that emerged after the death of Yuan Shikai. Leaders of this Clique were all from Anhui province. The faction headed by Duan Qirui. The political wing of the Anhui Clique was the Anfu Club |
| Ānhuī province | 安徽省 | Province in Eastern China |
| Anhui-Zhili War (Zhíwǎn Zhànzhēng) | 直皖战争 | July 14–23, 1920, a war between the Zhili and Anhui Cliques for control of the Beiyang government. Zhili was a northern province of China, where Beijing is physically located. During the Warlord Era the province was known as Zhili. After 1929, known as Hebei |

| Anti-Fèngtiān War | 反奉战争 | The last major intra-warlord conflict. It is also called the Third Zhílì-Fèngtiān War and Guominjun Fengtian War. Lasted Nov 1925 to April 1926 |
|---|---|---|
| Bái Chóngxǐ | 白崇禧 | Ethnic Hui Guangxi-born military great for the KMT side. Served as NRA chief of staff during the Northern Expedition. Lived from 1893-1966 |
| Bǎinián Guóchí | 百年国耻 | China's so-called "Century of Humiliation" that lasted from the Opium War to WWII |
| Bǎodìng Military Academy | 保定军校 | Another major military academy in China founded by Yuan Shikai |
| Bāotóu | 包头 | Major city in Inner Mongolia |
| Běipíng | 北平 | The name of Beijing for a brief while until the Communists changed it back in 1949 |
| Běiyáng | 北洋 | Literally "North Ocean Army." This army served as the centerpiece of the Qing Dynasty's military modernization efforts. |
| Běiyáng Army | 北洋军 | Literally "North Ocean Army." This army served as the centerpiece of the Qing Dynasty's military modernization efforts. |
| Běiyáng Clique | 北洋系 | The faction that arose out of the Beiyang Army. This army served as the centerpiece of the Qing Dynasty's military modernization efforts. |

| Běiyáng Fleet | 北洋艦隊 | The most powerful of China's four modern navies built up during the late Qing. Great, but not that great. |
|---|---|---|
| Běiyáng government | 北洋政府 | The northern Chinese faction comprised of all the top military figures from the Beiyang Army |
| Běiyáng Tōngshāng Dàchén | 北洋通商大臣 | Minister of Běiyáng |
| Bóhǎi Sea | 渤海湾 | A gulf located in the north Yellow Sea where Liaoning, Hebei and Shandong are all located |
| Cài È | 蔡锷 | 1882-1916, student of Liang Qichao Yunnan warlord, best known for his role in challenging the imperial ambitions of Yuan Shikai during the anti-monarchy war. |
| Cáo Kūn | 曹锟 | 1862-1938, Succeeded Feng Guozhang as head of the Zhili Clique, also former president of China |
| Cáo Kūn | 曹锟 | 1862-1938, Zhili Clique leader and president of China for a short time |
| Cháhā'ěr (Chahar) | 察哈尔 | Historic province from 1912-1936 just to the east of Suiyuan in what is today Inner Mongolia |
| Chángshā | 长沙 | Capital of Hunan |
| Chén Jiǒngmíng | 陈炯明 | Guangdong-born and raised Revolutionary. General and politician who lived from 1878-1933. Warlord of Guǎngdōng province and later rival to Sun Yat-sen |

| Chén Lìfū | 陈立夫 | He ran Chiang's Investigation Section of the KMT Organization Department |
|---|---|---|
| Chéngdé | 承德 | The city known in the modern Chinese history books as Jehol (Rehe). A popular summer residence of the Qing imperial court going back to Kangxi. |
| Chóngqìng | 重庆 | Used to be part of Sichuan, now an independent municipality. Also known as Chungking |
| Chǔ Yùpú | 褚玉璞 | 1887-1929, former Zhang Zuolin and Fengtian Clique stalwart. Also one of The Dogmeat Generals comrades |
| Cíxǐ | 慈禧太后 | The Empress Dowager Cixi, 1835-1908, ruled China from 1861 to 1908 |
| Dà Yuán Shuài | 大元帅 | generalissimo or grand marshal |
| Dài Lì | 戴笠 | The Himmler of China, head of Chiang Kai-shek's secret police organization |
| Dàlián | 大连 | Strategic port city in Liaoning Province where Port Arthur / Lushunkou located |
| Dèng Xiǎopíng | 邓小平 | 1904-1997, one of the greatest leaders of the 20th century and close ally of Chairman Mao (and paid a high price for that) |
| Dù Yuèshēng | 杜月笙 | 1888-1951, Big Eared Du, along with Pockmarked Huang, one of the top guys in the Green Gang that ruled the vice in Shanghai |

| | | |
|---|---|---|
| Duàn Qíruì | 段祺瑞 | 1865-1936. Warlord and China politician. Also served as premier. Originally from Hefei, Anhui, he headed the Anhui Clique |
| Dūdu | 都督 | Military governors in charge of civil administration |
| Dūjūn | 督军 | provincial military governors |
| Duke Huán of Qí | 齐桓公 | Rule of Qi State in Shandong from 685 to 643 BCE |
| Eastern Zhōu Dynasty | 东周 | Ran from approximately 770 to 256 BCE, comprising the second half of the Zhou Dynasty when the capital was at Luoyang. Also known as the Spring & Autumn and Warring States periods |
| Emperor Pǔyí | 溥仪 | The Last Emperor, also known as the Xuantong Emperor |
| Empress Dowager Cíxǐ | 慈禧太后 | The Empress Dowager Cixi, 1835-1908, ruled China from 1861 to 1908 |
| Empress Dowager Lóngyù | 孝定景皇后（隆裕） | 1868-1913, Former empress consort to the Guāngxù Emperor. Became Empress Dowager of the Qing following the death of Cixi in 1908 |
| Èrcì Gémìng | 二次革命 | The Second Revolution that lasted June to November 1913 |
| Fēicháng gǎnxiè nǐmen | 非常感谢你们 | I am extremely grateful to all of you |
| Féng Guózhāng | 冯国璋 | Zhili Clique leader after Yuan Shikai, general and politician during the Republic of China. Lived from 1859-1919 |

| | | |
|---|---|---|
| Féng Yùxiáng | 冯玉祥 | 1882-1948, known as The Christian Warlord and The Betraying General. A major figure from the warlord era |
| Fèngtiān Clique | 奉天系 | The faction headed by the Manchurian Warlord, Zhang Zuolin. One of the cliques that emerged after the death of Yuan Shikai. Leaders of this Clique were from Manchuria. Fengtian is an old name for Shenyang in Liaoning Province |
| First Zhílì-Fèngtiān War. | 第一次直奉战争 | April 1922-June 1922. War fought between the forces of Wu Peifu of the Zhili Clique against Zhang Zuolin of the Fengtian Clique. Wu Peifu prevailed. |
| Fújiàn | 福建 | Coastal province in southern China |
| Gānsù | 甘肃 | Western province of China. Capital is at Lanzhou |
| Gǒuròu Jiāngjūn | 狗肉将军 | The Dogmeat General, one of Zhang Zongchang's many nicknames |
| Guāndōng Army | 关东军 | Known in Japan as the Kantō-gun. They were a part of the Imperial Japanese Army and responsible for most of the atrocities carried out by Japan in China. |
| Guǎngdōng | 广东 | Province in Southern China |
| Guǎngxī | 广西 | Province in Southwest China next door to Guangdong |
| Guǎngxī Clique (Guì Xì) | 桂系 | One of the cliques that emerged after the death of Yuan Shikai. The leader of this Clique was Li Zongren |

| | | |
|---|---|---|
| Guāngxù Emperor | 光绪帝 | Second to last Qing Emperor who reigned from 1875-1908 |
| Guǎngzhōu | 广州 | Capital of Guangdong Province and major city in modern Chinese history (and ancient China too). Sun Yat-sen's base during the 1920's |
| Guìzhōu | 贵州 | Province in Southwest China |
| Guō Sōnglíng | 郭松龄 | 1883-1925, One of Zhang Zuolin's generals who mutinied in November 1925 which led to the Anti Fengtian War |
| Guómíndǎng | 国民党 | The KMT, known as the Kuomintang. The Nationalist Party |
| Guómínjūn | 国民军 | National People's Army. Also the name of Feng Yuxiang's Clique |
| Hǎichéng | 海城 | A city in Liaoning about midway between Shěnyáng and Dàlián... Liáoníng Province |
| Hàn Chinese | 汉族 | Ethnic Han Chinese, China's (and the world's) largest ethnic group. Also known as 华人 Hua Ren and 唐人 Tang Ren |
| Hàn Dynasty | 汉朝 | Ancient Chinese dynasty founded by Liu Bang that lasted from 206 BCE to 220 CE with a brief interregnum by Wang Mang from 9 CE to 23 CE |
| Hànkǒu | 汉口 | One of the three cities that makes up the metropolis of Wuhan (Hanyang and Wuchang being the other two) |
| Hànyáng | 汉阳 | One of the three cities that makes up the metropolis of Wuhan (Hankou and Wuchang being the other two) |

| | | |
|---|---|---|
| Harbin | 哈尔滨 | Capital of Heilongjiang Province in Manchuria |
| Hé Yìngqīn | 何应钦 | 1890-1987, general and politician in the Republic of China as well as a close Chiang Kai-shek ally |
| Héběi | 河北 | Northern province of China, where Beijing is physically located. During the Warlord Era the province was known as Zhili |
| Héféi | 合肥 | Capital of Anhui Province |
| Hēilóngjiāng | 黑龙江省 | One of the three provinces of Manchuria. Capital is Harbin |
| Hénán | 河南省 | Ancient province of China on the central plain. Capital is Zhengzhou |
| Hóng Húzi | 红胡子 | Red Beards, the roving militias of the north of China |
| Hóng Qiāng Huì | 红枪会 | The Red Spears Society |
| Hóng Xiùquán | 洪秀全 | 1814-1864, a Hakka revolutionary who led the Taiping Rebellion against the Qing Dynasty. Known as the Taiping Heavenly King |
| Hóngxiàn Emperor | 洪宪 | The regnal name of Yuan Shikai during his short-lived bid to become emperor |
| Hú Hànmín | 胡汉民 | 1879-1936, on again off again ally of Chiang Kai-shek. A major political figure in the KMT from the earliest days |

| Huái Army | 淮军 | Named after China's Huai River. Also called the Anhui Army. It was led by Li Hongzhang and later became part of the New Army and later, the Beiyang Army |
|---|---|---|
| Huáng Jīnróng | 黄金荣 | 1868-1953, known as Pockmarked Huáng. He, along with his cohorts, most famously Big Ears Du Yuesheng, ran the Green Gang, the most powerful criminal organization in Shanghai |
| Huánggūtún Shìjàn | 皇姑屯事件 | The event that happened June 4, 1928 when rogue elements from the Guandong Army blew up Zhang Zuolin's train as it approached Huanggutun Station in Shenyang |
| Huángpǔ Jūnxiào | 黄埔军校 | Whampoa Military Academy |
| Húběi | 湖北 | Central Chinese province where Wuhan is located |
| Hùfǎ Yùndòng | 护法运动 | Movement to Protect the Constitution |
| Hùfǎjūn | 护法军 | The Constitutional Protection Army who fought against (and lost to) the northern warlords |
| Hùguó Zhànzhēng | 护国战争 | The National Protection War directed against Yuan Shikai. December 1915 to July 1916 |
| Hūhéhàotè | 呼和浩特 | Hohhet, capital of Inner Mongolia |
| Húnán | 湖南 | Province in central China, capital is Changsha |

| | | |
|---|---|---|
| Húnán | 湖南 | Province in south central China woth its capital at Changsha |
| Jiāngsū | 江苏 | Coastal Province in East China north of Shanghai |
| Jiāngxī | 江西 | Province in Eastern China |
| Jiāngxī Soviet | 中央革命根据地 | Also known as the Jiangxi-Fujian Soviet. Lasted from 1931 to 1934. |
| Jílín | 吉林 | The third province that makes up the region of Manchuria |
| Jìn | 晋 | Ancient state during the Western Zhou period. Its location was in and around where present day Shanxi is located. |
| Jìnán | 济南 | Capital city of Shandong Province |
| Jǐnggāngshān | 井冈山 | City in southwest Jiangxi province where mountains are located that served as Mao's base during the early 30's. |
| Jiǔ Yī Bā | 九一八 | A staged incident that happened in Shenyang September 18, 1931 used by Japan to invade and control northeast China. Also known as the Mukden or Manchurian Incident |
| Jūnfá | 军阀 | Warlord |
| Kāng Yǒuwéi | 康有为 | 1858-1927, scholar official known for his reforming efforts during the late Qing Dynasty |
| Kǒng Xiángxǐ | 孔祥熙 | H.H. Kung, KMT stalwart, finance minister, and spouse to one of the Soong Sisters, the oldest and brightest, Aìlíng |

| | | |
|---|---|---|
| Láizhōu | 莱州 | City located on the north Shāndōng coast west of Yāntái |
| Lǐ Dàzhāo | 李大钊 | 1889-1927, co-founder of the Chinese Communist Party and a major intellectual of his day. Killed by Zhang Zuolin's forces |
| Lǐ Hóngzhāng | 李鸿章 | 1823-1901, Qing era general, diplomat and politician |
| Lǐ Lièjūn | 李烈钧 | 1882-1946, Chinese revolutionary leader and general in the early Republic of China |
| Lí Yuánhóng | 黎元洪 | Lived 1864-1928, president of the ROC 1916-1917 and 1922-23 |
| Lǐ Zōngrén | 李宗仁 | 1890-1969, Guangxi Warlord who later served as Vice president and president of the Republic of China |
| Liáng Qǐchāo | 梁启超 | 1873-1929, Chinese man of letters as well as a political figure of the late Qing and early ROC periods |
| Liáng Shìyí | 梁士诒 | Lived from 1869-1933. Old Yuan Shikai ally who served as premier of the republic for one month |
| Liáoníng province | 辽宁省 | One of the three provinces of Manchuria, was known as Fèngtiān province for about a quarter century |
| Lín Yǔtáng | 林语堂 | 1895-1976, Chinese linguist and writer, considered by many to be the greatest of the 20th century. He had a brilliant academic career and was a major influence on key leaders. |

| | | |
|---|---|---|
| Lín Zéxú | 林则徐 | 1785-1850 Viceroy of Guangdong-Guangzi, famous for standing up to the foreign powers in the early stages of the Opium War conflict |
| Liú Bāng | 刘邦 | Founder of the Han Dynasty who defeated Xiang Yu in the Chu-Han Contention. Also known as Han Gaozu, he lived from approximately 256-195 BCE |
| Liú Zhēnnián | 刘珍年 | 1898-1935, One of Zhang Zongchang's close generals, later a warlord in his own right. Known also as "The Killer" |
| Lǔ | 鲁 | Ancient state in Shandong with its capital at Qufu. Lu was also the birthplace of Confucius |
| Lù Róngtíng | 陆荣廷 | Guangxi warlord who lived from 1859-1928. Headed what was known as the "Old Guangxi Clique" |
| Lú Yǒngxiáng | | Military governor of Zhèjiāng and was an Ānhuī Clique man. Lived from 1867 to 1933 |
| Luòyáng | 洛阳 | Former ancient capital of several dynasties. Located in historic Henan Province |
| Mǎ Clique. | 马家军 | The Muslim warlords of northwest China (Qinghai, Gansu, Ningxia). The four primary warlords were Ma Bufang , Ma Hongkui, Ma Hongbin and Ma Buqing |
| Mǎfū | 马夫 | Called a Mafoo, a kind of horse groom who worked in the stables |

| | | |
|---|---|---|
| Manchukuo (Mǎnzhōuguó) | 满洲国 | Japanese Puppet state setup in Manchuria in 1932 |
| Máo Zédōng | 毛泽东 | 1893-1976, Great 20th century revolutionary who ruled China from its founding in 1949 till his death in 1976. Responsible for a lot of death, among other things. |
| Měilíng Gōng | 美龄宫 | The beautiful residence in the mountains of Fenghua County in Xikou where Chiang and Madame Chiang shared a villa |
| Miáo Rebellion | 苗乱 | The third of three rebellions centered in Guizhou Province that lasted 1854-1873 |
| Mófàn Dūjūn | 模范督军 | Yan Xishan's nickname: The Model Governor |
| Mukden Incident | 九一八事变 | Also known as The Manchurian Incident. A staged incident that happened in Shenyang September 18, 1931 used by Japan to invade and control northeast China. Also known as the Manchurian Incident |
| Nánchāng | 南昌 | Capital of Jiangxi province |
| Nánjīng | 南京 | Capital of Jiangsu province, the Republic of China and seat of Chiang Kai-shek's government |
| Niǎn Rebellion | 捻乱 | Major peasant uprising in China that lasted 1851-1868. |
| Níngbō | 宁波 | Coastal city in Zhejiang Province |
| Níngbō rén | 宁波人 | Someone from Ningbo |
| Ordos | 鄂尔多斯 | City in Inner Mongolia |

| Pénglái | 蓬莱 | City in Shandong |
|---|---|---|
| Pǔyí | 溥仪 | The Last Emperor, also known as the Xuantong Emperor |
| Qí | 齐国 | During ancient times Qi was a kingdom in Shandong with its capital at Linzi |
| Qí Xièyuán | 齐燮元 | 1885-1946, Military governor in Jiāngsū and also was a Zhílì Clique member and ally of Wu Peifu. Later executed in 1946 as a Japanese collaborator |
| Qiānggǎnzi lǐmiàn chū zhèngquán | 枪杆子里面出政权 | Political power grows out of the barrel of a gun, as said by Mao Zedong in 1927 and later in 1938 |
| Qiánlóng Emperor | 乾隆帝 | Qing dynasty emperor who reigned 1735-1796 |
| Qín Shǐhuáng | 秦始皇 | Qin Dynasty founder and unifier of the nation |
| Qing Dynasty | 清朝 | China's last imperial dynasty, lasted 1644-1911 |
| Qīngcháo mòniándé mònián | 清朝末年的末年 | No one actually ever says this but the Mònián usually mean the final years (of a dynasty). So the Mònián de mònián mean the last years of the last years of the dynasty |
| Qínhuángdǎo | 秦皇岛 | Coastal city in northeast Hebei, located right where the Great Wall starts at Shanhaiguan |
| Sān Bù Zhī Jiāngjūn | 三不知将军 | "Three Don't Knows" General |

| Second Zhílì Fèngtiān War | 第二次直奉战争 | September to November 1924. The second war between the two powerful cliques of Fengtian led by Zhang Zuolin and Zhili les by Cao Kun and Wu Peifu |
|---|---|---|
| Shāndōng | 山东 | Coastal province in North China |
| Shāng | 商 | China's earliest dynasty for which their is recorded evidence (in the Oracle Bones). This ancient dynasty lasted from about the 1500's BCE to 1046 BCE. |
| Shānhǎiguān | 山海关 | Located around Qinhuangdao, Hebei province. Shanhai Pass. The part of the Great Wall built by Qi Jiguang during the Ming either begins at Shanhaiguan or terminates there. Shanhaiguan is located less than 200 miles from Beijing |
| Shǎnxī | 陕西省 | Northern province of China. Xian (ancient Chang'an) is the capital. |
| Shǎnxī | 陕西 | Province in north central China where Xian is located |
| Shānxī | 山西省 | Northern province of China. Taiyuan is the capital. |
| Shānxī Clique | 晋系 | One of the cliques that emerged after the death of Yuan Shikai. The leader of this Clique was Yan Xishan |
| Shěnyáng | 沈阳 | Capital city in Liaoning province |
| Shī Cóngbīn | 施从滨 | Commander in Sun Chuanfang's army. Executed by Sun |
| Shī Jiànqiào | 施剑翘 | Daughter of Shi Congbin and Sun Chuanfang's executioner |

| Sòng | 宋朝 | Dynasty that lasted (in two parts) from 960-1279 |
|------|------|------|
| Sòng Jiàorén | 宋教仁 | 1882-1913, Chinese republican revolutionary, political leader and a founder of the Kuomintang (KMT). He was assassinated in 1913 after leading his Kuomintang party to victory in China's first democratic elections. |
| Sòng Měilíng | 宋美龄 | 1897-2003 (lived to 105!!) Madame Chiang Kai-shek |
| Suí | 隋朝 | Dynasty in China that lasted 581-618 |
| Súiyuǎn | 绥远 | A historic province in the central part of present-day Inner Mongolia |
| Sūn Chuánfāng | 孙传芳 | 1885-1935, Shandong-born military man known as the "Nanking Warlord." Part of the Zhili Clique |
| Sun Yat sen | 孙逸仙 | Called the "Father of Modern China." A revolutionary, statesman and KMT founder. Lived from 1866-1925 |
| Sūnzǐ | 孙子 | 6th century BCE general and military strategist known in Tinseltown as Sun-Tzu and known for his masterwork "The Art of War" |
| Tài Shān | 泰山 | Mount Tai, one of the Five Great Mountains of China (The 五岳) |
| Tàiháng | 太行山 | 250 mile long mountain range in Shanxi, Henan and Hebei |
| Tàipíng Rebellion | 太平天国运动 | Rebellion and civil war in China that lasted from 1850-1864 |
| Tàiyuán | 太原 | Capital of Shanxi and the province's largest city |

| | | |
|---|---|---|
| Táng | 唐朝 | Dynasty that lasted 618-907 |
| Táng Jìyáo | 唐继尧 | 1883-1927, general and warlord of Yunnan during the Warlord Era of early Republican China. He was military governor of Yunnan from 1913-27 |
| Táng Shàoyí | 唐绍仪 | Chinese diplomat and statesman. Lived from 1862-1938 |
| Táng Shēngzhì | 唐生智 | 1889-1970, Hunan born warlord who later joined Chiang Kai-shek's side |
| Tàipíng Rebellion. | 太平天国 | Rebellion and civil war in China that lasted from 1850-1864 |
| Tiānjìn | 天津 | Municipality within Hebei Province but reporting direct to the Central Government. Just southeast of Beijing |
| Tianjin Military Academy | 天津军校 | Military Academy founded by Li Hongzhang |
| Tiānxia Dìyīguān | 天下第一关 | "The First Barrier under Heaven" as the Great Wall is called at Shanhaiguan |
| Tóng Chuáng Yì Mèng | 同床异梦 | Old Chinese saying that means, "Same bed, different dreams" |
| Tóngménghuì | 同盟会 | Sun Yat-sen's United League, forerunner to the Guomindang 国民党....or KMT. |
| Treaty of Shimonoseki | 下关条约 | Also known as the 马关条约, signed on April 17, 1895. It ended the First Sino- Japanese War |
| Viceroy of Zhílì | 直隶总督 | The leader of Zhili Province. Held by Zheng Guofan, Li Hongzhang and Yuan Shikai. This viceroy held huge sway over the government in Beijing |

| Wǎn Xì | 皖系 | Ānhuī Clique |
|---|---|---|
| Wáng Chǒnghuì | 王宠惠 | 1881-1958, Close associate of Sun Yat-sen. Chinese diplomat and politician from 1912 to 1958. |
| Wāng Jīngwèi | 汪精卫 | 1883-1944, controversial KMT leader who first led the Leftists and later became an anti-Communist. Foe of Chiang Kai-shek |
| Wáng Mǎng | 王莽 | Han Dynasty official who seized the throne and ruled as emperor of the Xin Dynasty 9-23 CE |
| Wáng Zhànyuán | 王占元 | 1861-1934, Chinese general and warlord of Hubei province (Featured in Part 4 of this Warlord series) |
| Wǎn xì | 皖系 | The Ānhuī Clique |
| Wellington Koo | 顾维钧 | 1926-1927, Republic of China statesman, diplomat and representative at the Paris Peace Conference 1919. |
| Western Jìn | 西晋 | Ancient dynasty that lasted from 266-316 |
| Whampoa Military Academy | 黄埔军校 | Military academy opened in May 1924. Chiang Kai-shek was the commandant |
| Wú Pèifú | 吴佩孚 | 1862-1938, Succeeded Feng Guozhang as head of the Zhili Clique, also former president of China |
| Wǔchāng | 武昌 | The third of the three cities that makes up the metropolis of Wuhan. Also the site of the Wuchang Uprising 10-10-1911 |

| | | |
|---|---|---|
| Wǔchāng Uprising | 武昌起义 | Uprising that started on 10-10-1911 in the city of Wuchang. Led to the fall of the Qing Dynasty |
| Wūhǎi | 乌海 | City in Inner Mongolia |
| Wǔhàn | 武汉 | City in Hubei made up of Wuchang, Hankou and Hanyang |
| Wǔsān Cǎn'àn | 五三惨案 | Jinan Incident, May 3, 1928 |
| Wǔtái | 五台山 | Mountains in northeast Shanxi. One of them is sacred |
| Xì | 系 | clique or faction |
| Xià Dynasty | 夏朝 | Ancient mythical dynasty that ran from 2070-1600 BCE and was succeeded by the Shang Dynasty |
| Xīān Incident (Xīān Shìbiàn) | 西安事变 | Happened December 12-26, 1936 in Xian. Zhang Xueliang's crazy attempt to force Chiang Kai-shek to join with the CCP to fight Japan |
| Xiánfēng Emperor | 咸丰帝 | Qing emperor who reigned 1850-1861 |
| Xiāng Army | 湘军 | Army organized and led by Zeng Guofan. It saw action during the Taiping Rebellion |
| Xiàng Yǔ | 项羽 | Warrior King of Chu State (modern-day Hubei) who lived from 232-202 BCE. He faced Liu Bang unsuccessfully to become a unifying emperor of China |
| Xīběi Sān Mǎ | 西北三吗 | Old CHP episode 78...The Warlord Ma Clique of Northwest China |
| Xīkǒu | 溪口 | City outside of Ningbo where Chiang Kai-shek was born |

| | | |
|---|---|---|
| Xīn Jūn | 新军 | The New Army, short for Xīnjiàn Lùjūn. 新建陆军. Later became the Beiyang Army |
| Xīnhài Revolution | 辛亥革命 | The Revolution of 1911 which climaxed in the Wuchang Uprising on October 10th |
| Xīnjiāng | 新疆 | China's northwestern province located north of Tibet and south of Russia and Mongolia |
| Xīnzhōu | 忻州 | City in northern Shanxi. Hometown of Yan Xishan |
| Xú Shìchāng | 徐世昌 | Beiyang Clique stalwart going back to the beginning. Lived from 1855-1939. Not a military man. Served as both president and premier of the Republic of China |
| Xúzhōu | 徐州 | City in northern Jiāngsū where it meets the borders of Ānhuī and Shāndōng. |
| Yán Xīshān | 閻錫山 | 1883-1960, the Shanxi Warlord, he ran things in Shanxi for thirty-eight years. |
| Yángzǐjiāng | 扬子江 | The Yangzi River |
| Yāntái | 烟台 | City in Northeast Shandong |
| Yáo | 尧 | Mythical ancient emperor who lived from 2333-2234 BCE. He was one of the Three Sovereigns and Five Emperors |
| Yíchāng | 宜昌 | Major city in Hubei, second largest after Wuhan |

| Yǒng Yíng | 勇营 | Also known as Braves, these were regional militias that emerged during the Qing that consisted of local peasant soldiers |
|---|---|---|
| Yǔ the Great | 大禹 | Mythical founder of the Xià Dynasty. Lived from 2123-2025 BCE, or so says Sima Qian |
| Yuán Shìkǎi. | 袁世凯 | 1859-1916, Military and government official and first president of the Republic of China. Also called "The First Warlord" |
| Yúnnán | 云南 | A province in southwestern China known for its large number of ethnic minorities |
| Zēng Guófān | 曾国藩 | 1811-1872, Qing era statesman, general, scholar and leader of the Xiang (Hunan) Army. |
| Zhāng Qún | 张群 | 1889-1990, another longtime ally of Chiang Kai-shek who served as one of his most trusted generals. Also served as premier |
| Zhāng Xuéliáng | 张学良 | The Young Marchal, son of Zhang Zuolin. Lived a hundred years from June 3, 1901 to October 15, 2001 |
| Zhāng Xūn | 张勋 | 1854-1923, Qing loyalist general who attempted to restore the abdicated emperor Puyi in the Manchu Restoration of 1917. He also supported Yuan Shikai during his time as president |

| | | |
|---|---|---|
| Zhāng Zōngchāng | 张宗昌 | Known affectionately as The Dogmeat General, also known by many nicknames, he was one of Zhang Zuolin's best generals. Later became Military Governor of Shandong. Lived from 1881-1932 |
| Zhāng Zuòlín | 张作霖 | 1875-1928, Liaoning-born warlord of Manchuria and major political figure as well. Also served as President of the ROC. |
| Zhāng Zuòlín | 张作霖 | 1875-1928, The Manchurian Warlord, another major warlord in his day. He headed the Fengtian Clique |
| Zhāngjiākǒu | 張家口 | City located to the northwest of Beijing, also known in Chinese history by its Mongol name, Kalgan |
| Zhèjiāng | 浙江 | Coastal Province in Central China |
| Zhèng Jìchéng | 郑继成 | son of Zheng Jicheng and executioner of Zhang Zongchang |
| Zhèng Jīnshēng | 郑金声 | Military general executed by Zhang Zongchang in 1927 |
| Zhèngzhōu | 郑州 | Major city in Henan Province |
| Zhí Xì | 直系 | Zhílì Clique |
| Zhílì | 直隶 | Ming and Qing era province that today mostly comprises Hebei |
| Zhílì Ānhuī War | 直皖 战争 | July 14-23, 1920, war between Zhili and Anhui Cliques for control of the Beiyang government |

| Zhílì Clique | 直系 | The assemblage of mostly Hebei-based militarists and politicians. Their leader was Feng Guozhang. And upon Feng's death, the Zhili Clique was led by Cao Kun and Wu Peifu |
|---|---|---|
| Zhílì province | 直隶省 | Former name of Hebei province |
| Zhílì-Ānhuī War (Zhí-Wǎn Zhànzhēng) | 直皖战争 | Fought between the forces of Cáo Kūn and Wú Pèifú on the Zhili side defeating Duàn Qíruì's Ānhuī Army in 1920 |
| Zhílì-Fèngtiān War | 直奉战争 | The First Zhili Fengtian War was fought April 1922-June 1922 between the forces of Wu Peifu of the Zhili Clique against Zhang Zuolin of the Fengtian Clique. Wu Peifu prevailed. |
| Zhōng diǎnzhàn | 终点站 | The final stop (on a route) |
| Zhōngtiáo | 中条山 | Mountain range in southern Shanxi |
| Zhōu Dynasty | 周朝 | Western Zhou 1046-771 BCE and Eastern Zhou 771-221 BCE |
| Zhōu Ēnlái | 周恩来 | 1898-1976, First Premier of the PRC. Served up until his death in 1976. Check out the eight-part series on his life |
| Zǒng Dū | 总督 | Viceroy or governor-general |

Printed by Libri Plureos GmbH in Hamburg, Germany